Cambridge Elements

Elements in Public Economics
edited by
Robin Boadway
Queen's University
Frank A. Cowell
The London School of Economics and Political Science
Massimo Florio
University of Milan

THE MARGINAL COST OF PUBLIC FUNDS

Per-Olov Johansson
Stockholm School of Economics

Bengt Kriström
SLU-Umeå

CAMBRIDGE
UNIVERSITY PRESS

Shaftesbury Road, Cambridge CB2 8EA, United Kingdom

One Liberty Plaza, 20th Floor, New York, NY 10006, USA

477 Williamstown Road, Port Melbourne, VIC 3207, Australia

314–321, 3rd Floor, Plot 3, Splendor Forum, Jasola District Centre,
New Delhi – 110025, India

103 Penang Road, #05–06/07, Visioncrest Commercial, Singapore 238467

Cambridge University Press is part of Cambridge University Press & Assessment,
a department of the University of Cambridge.

We share the University's mission to contribute to society through the pursuit of
education, learning and research at the highest international levels of excellence.

www.cambridge.org
Information on this title: www.cambridge.org/9781009620475

DOI: 10.1017/9781009620437

First published 2025

A catalogue record for this publication is available from the British Library

ISBN 978-1-009-62047-5 Hardback
ISBN 978-1-009-62048-2 Paperback
ISSN 2516-2276 (online)
ISSN 2516-2268 (print)

Cambridge University Press & Assessment has no responsibility for the persistence
or accuracy of URLs for external or third-party internet websites referred to in this
publication and does not guarantee that any content on such websites is, or will
remain, accurate or appropriate.

For EU product safety concerns, contact us at Calle de José Abascal, 56, 1°, 28003
Madrid, Spain, or email eugpsr@cambridge.org

The Marginal Cost of Public Funds

Elements in Public Economics

DOI: 10.1017/9781009620437
First published online: May 2025

Per-Olov Johansson
Stockholm School of Economics

Bengt Kriström
SLU-Umeå

Author for correspondence: Per-Olov Johansson, per-olov.johansson@hhs.se

Abstract: In a perfect market economy, the cost of raising another euro of tax revenue equals one. However, once distortionary taxes on goods and factors are introduced, the marginal cost of public funds, MCPF, typically deviates from one. Often it exceeds one, but one can also find cases where it falls short of one. This Element introduces the concept of the MCPF, sketches its history, and discusses a number of applications. It does this by undertaking economic evaluations of public sector projects involving a pure public good. An important distinction in the literature relates to where the government has access to lump-sum taxation versus where it must rely on changing a distortionary tax. These are often unit taxes or proportional taxes. Sometimes they are even introduced to alleviate a problem. An example is a tax on emissions of greenhouse gases. This title is also available as Open Access on Cambridge Core.

Keywords: marginal cost of public funds, social marginal cost of public funds, marginal excess burden, cost–benefit analysis, emission taxes

JEL classifications: D04, D31, D50, D60, D61, D62, H20, H21, H23, H41, H53

ISBNs: 9781009620475 (HB), 9781009620482 (PB), 9781009620437 (OC)
ISSNs: 2516-2276 (online), 2516-2268 (print)

Contents

1	Introduction	1
2	Notes on the History of the MCPF	3
3	The MCPF under Lump-Sum Taxation	6
4	Ramsey Taxation	18
5	A Smörgåsbord of Further Topics in Variations of the Basic Model	24
6	Extension to a World with Many Goods and Factors and to an Intertemporal World	41
7	Optimal and Nonoptimal Income Distributions	48
8	A Few Reflections on Empirical Approaches	56
	Appendix	61
	References	73

1 Introduction

In a perfect market economy, the cost of raising an additional euro to finance the government's spending is equal to one. However, once distortionary taxes are introduced, the marginal cost of public funds, MCPF or MCF, typically deviates from one. The MCPF is a concept that has been around for a long time. However, many different interpretations are available. Therefore, Section 2 of this Element is devoted to a brief historical review, from Adam Smith in the eighteenth century via Dupuit and Marshall in the nineteenth century to the most recent contributions.

As is noted in Section 2, the MCPF has far-reaching implications across a wide range of policy issues. However, in the rest of this Element, the focus is on the role of the MCPF in economic evaluations. An obvious approach to the derivation of concepts for the (social) marginal cost of public funds is to maximize a social welfare function subject to one or several constraints. Typically, the project whose welfare contribution is maximized provides a pure public good; see, for example, Auerbach and Hines (2002), Bastani (2023), Gahvari (2006), and Jacobs (2018). However, this Element mostly takes a more "applied" approach and looks at how a small or marginal project affects monetary welfare, although a few maximization problems are discussed. The reason is that the chosen approach probably is more straightforward for a cost–benefit practitioner than the solution to a constrained optimization problem. Initially, the focus is on extremely simple economies. This approach illuminates the principal composition of the concept of the MCPF and illustrates its role in a cost–benefit analysis (CBA).

There is a slightly different approach from CBA that is termed the Marginal Value of Public Funds, MVPF; refer to Hendren and Sprung-Keyser (2020, pp. 1222–24) for a comparison of this concept and a traditional CBA. Hendren and Sprung-Keyser (2020, p. 1224) note, "Despite our advocacy for the value of the MVPF over a traditional cost-benefit analysis, it is perhaps reassuring to note that, in most cases, these two approaches generate similar conclusions." In Subsection 3.3 we introduce a simple variation of the concept and compare it to a "conventional" CBA and the benefit–cost ratio.

Following Lundholm (2005) another concept is termed the *social* marginal cost of public funds, SMCPF, which uses a slightly different "exchange rate" between units of utility and monetary units, as is illuminated in Subsection 3.4. A potential problem with the concept is highlighted. As applied by Jacobs (2018), monetary benefits are measured in one "currency" while monetary costs are valued in another currency (with an unknown "exchange rate" between the two). Utility benefits are converted to monetary units using the private marginal utility of income. In contrast, utility costs are converted using the social marginal utility of income (that accounts for the impact of income effects on tax bases). However, as we show, if correctly undertaken, the approach will reduce to a conventional CBA.

There is another use of what is termed the SMCPF. In a multi-household economy, the SMCPF is a sum of individual marginal costs of public funds that are multiplied by distributional weights. Refer to, for example, Bessho and Hayashi (2013). Distributional concerns are addressed in Section 7 of this Element.

The simple approach taken in the first sections of this Element is also useful in addressing another "competing" concept to the MCPF, namely the MEB, of taxation and to illustrate how the MEB is related to the MCPF. The approach employed in computable general equilibrium, CGE, models approximates an MEB by calculating the willingness to pay, WTP, to avoid a small tax increase divided by the associated change in tax revenue. This approach results in the problem that as the tax change is made smaller, one ultimately ends up in 0/0.

The chosen approach also allows us to check how the MCPF is affected by different "parameters," such as price changes, social security fees, revenues earned by the project, unemployment, and what the concept looks like if a private actor runs the considered project.

Sometimes, the MCPF is defined independently of specific projects. This might seem reasonable, as it allows for separating the MCPF from individual project considerations. However, this is no problem-free approach. In particular, if the project under consideration does not constitute part of the government's budget, why adjust the project's costs by an MCPF? The general equilibrium foundations of the approach are far from self-evident, as is illuminated in Subsection A.5 of the Appendix. Another difference is that a definition based on a project assumes that there is a tax, which is a function of the considered project, and adjusts to balance the government's budget. Without a project, the tax change can be exogenous, and the resulting surplus is stored or wasted. Finally, as is demonstrated already in Sections 3 and 4, in evaluating a project, the adjusted tax need not fall on an input used (or an output provided) by the project under evaluation. Nevertheless, we provide in Subsection 4.4 and Subsection A.2 of the Appendix digestion of the MCPF when there is no project.

Although the focus is on simple models, Section 6 introduces many goods and factors and an intertemporal world. Section 7 addresses the case with many agents, i.e., discusses distributional issues. The final and short section is devoted to a brief review of empirical approaches to estimating the MCPF.

There are virtually an infinite number of combinations of different taxes that can be used to finance a project. Only a selection of these combinations can be covered in this Element. A couple of omitted cases deserve to be mentioned. The hypothesis maintained in this Element is that most practitioners base discounting on the social rate of time preference. This justifies that decisions based on concepts like the social opportunity cost of capital are ignored. Such approaches typically draw on either sophisticated optimal control theory or dynamic programming. The alternative to a project is an investment rather than a tax increase, eliminating the need for an explicit MCPF consideration. The reader interested in reading about taxing capital is referred to Hashimzade and Myles (2014), Chapters 7–8 in Dahlby (2008) and Sørensen (2011, 2014). However, in Subsection 5.4, a tax on profit income is introduced and used to finance the considered public sector project. In contrast, Subsection 5.5 considers a private-sector project in a tax-distorted economy. Another omission refers to risk handling. A good overview of the field is provided by Smith (2022). An (2023) highlights the important impact of charitable giving and warm glow, i.e., non-welfarist approaches, on identifying the MCPF.

It is not necessary to raise taxes to finance a public sector project. An option is to displace other public sector activities. Because the aim is to look at the MCPF, this option is not considered in this Element. A discussion of what might be termed the marginal cost of public sector projects is found in Johansson and Kriström (2019).

The Element is structured as follows. Section 2 provides notes on the history of the MCPF. Section 3 considers the MCPF when lump-sum taxation is used to finance a project, but there also are fixed distortionary taxes on a good and labor. The concept of the social marginal utility of income, a competing concept to the private marginal utility of income, is also addressed. Section 4 abandons the assumption that lump-sum taxation can be used to finance projects and also looks at the concept of the MEB of taxation. Section 5 addresses diverse cases to highlight how different factors affect the MCPF. Section 6 generalizes the approach to an arbitrary number of goods and factors and an intertemporal world. Thus far, there is a single representative agent in the models. Section 7 discusses a few (non-Mirrlees and Mirrlees) multi-agent models to shed some light on how the MCPF is modified if there is an arbitrary number of agents. Section 8 provides a few thoughts on how to estimate the MCPF empirically. An Appendix is added. It provides further details of some of the issues dealt with in the Element.

2 Notes on the History of the MCPF

The ideas that led to the development of the MCPF can, perhaps not surprisingly, be traced back to "The Wealth of Nations" (Smith, 1776, Ch 2, Part II). In his discourse on the nature of taxation and public expenditure, Smith posited that taxes "ought to be designed as to take out of the pockets of the people as little as possible, over and above what it brings into the public treasury of the state." It seems clear that Smith was aware of what we today call deadweight loss. There was a cost of the tax "over and above" what a consumer had to pay for public services. At the time of his writing, there were, however, no tools available to measure that cost.

As pointed out by Musgrave (1987, p. 1059), the introduction of consumer surplus by Dupuit (1844) – further developed by Marshall (1890) – made it possible to rigorously measure the welfare loss imposed by different taxation schemes.[1] Developments of microeconomic theory in the twentieth century helped to clarify the MCPF concept, as well as suggested rigorous measurement approaches. The MCPF became a tool for evaluating the efficiency of tax policies.

However, the history of welfare measurement related to taxation started with the closely related concept of EB. In his survey of the literature, Boehne (1968) credits the first rigorous economic analysis of EB (using indifference curves) with Barone (1912). The literature then mostly circled around the pros and cons of direct versus indirect taxation, in a partial equilibrium setting. A key contribution, according to Boehne (1968, p. 25) was Joseph (1939), who generalized Marshall, Hicks, and other frameworks available at the time. She studied the welfare economics of taxation and helped decrease its dependency (Boehne, 1968, p. 25) on a priori assumptions about (zero) price and income elasticities, including relaxing the "Marshallian" assumption of a constant marginal utility of money.

The next important step was to move from partial to general equilibrium analysis, with key contributions by Arnold Harberger, for example, Harberger (1964). He showed how the analysis could be undertaken empirically in an ex-ante tax-ridden economy. In Harberger's own words "...in the general equilibrium case you take account of preexisting distortions that are affected by your move, and if you're just doing partial equilibrium, you don't." (Harberger and Just, 2012, p. 11). The general equilibrium perspective proved essential for a deeper understanding of the MCPF in empirical applications.

The MCPF concept, as understood today, is often attributed to Pigou (1948). He identified two types of costs with the tax system; administration and compliance together with what he called an "indirect damage" inflicted on the

---

[1] While Dupuit is generally regarded as the father of consumer surplus and other welfare economics concept, Vickrey (1968, p. 311) argues that "Thus, although Dupuit must clearly be given priority in the formulation of some of the fundamental concepts of modern welfare economics, his work appears to have had singularly little actual influence on the way economic thought developed over the next century."

consumer beyond the costs of paying the tax. Administrative costs are the expenses incurred by the government to collect taxes, including the cost of running tax offices, paying salaries to the staff, and maintaining the technology infrastructure required for tax collection. Compliance costs cover expenses borne by taxpayers to comply with tax laws. His analysis has been interpreted to mean that he thought that the MCPF was greater than one.

A key contribution to the early literature on the MCPF was William Vickrey. He applied his ideas to the New York subway deficit in the 1950s, which would be covered by the city budget by increasing taxes. He estimated the cost of this financing to be 130 cents to the dollar. He compared this to alternative fare structures (pricing above marginal cost) that would imply welfare losses of less than 30 cents per dollar. As explained by Atkinson et al. (1997, p. 194) "…he seeks to precisely to implement the Ramsey conditions – but not against a fixed budget constraint; against a fixed MCPF, which is in principle a superior criterion (since it amounts to choosing optimally the level of the constraint)." Vickrey's contribution stresses the importance of considering the full economic impact of taxation beyond the immediate revenue generated.

The literature has developed in various directions since Vickrey's seminal work. Only a few examples are provided here. Gahvari (2006), building on Samuelson (1954) and Mirrlees (1971) provides a tax model with heterogeneous agents (see section 7). He argues that tax policy should consider both the benefits of public goods and the diverse impacts of funding them on different agents. His analysis challenges, among other things, Pigou's assertion that distortive taxation warrants a reduced supply of public goods (in modern terms, when MCPF > 1). For a summary of the optimal taxation literature that discusses Pigou's assertion, see Tuomala (2016).

Hashimzade and Myles (2014) expand the Barro endogenous growth model and discuss how the composition of public spending and the structure of taxation affect long-term economic growth. Earlier contributions had mainly focused on public spending as an aggregate. They showed that the composition of spending could make a difference in long-run growth. Spending on infrastructure or education may bolster productivity and, thereby, economic growth.

Part of the more recent literature deals with specific challenges, such as sector characteristics, informal economies, "green" double dividends, and tax evasion by multinationals. A few examples of this development follow.

Chetty et al. (2009) demonstrated that the economic incidence of a tax depends not only on statutory incidence but also on how salient the tax is to consumers. For instance, sales taxes included in the price (low salience) may generate smaller behavioral responses compared to taxes added at the point of sale (high salience), even if the monetary amounts are identical.

Cordano and Balistreri (2010) use a computable equilibrium model with data on Peru, showing that the cost of raising public funds can differ significantly depending on sector-specific characteristics. Sectors with inelastic demand, rigid supply constraints, or limited competition may face higher MCPFs, thereby influencing optimal tax policy design across sectors.

Auriol and Warlters (2012) include the informal economy in the general equilibrium assessment of the MCPF in 38 African countries, suggesting that the informal economy provides a relatively low-cost source of tax revenue. They also find a significant variation of the MCPF in different countries implying that a one-size-fits-all approach to taxation may not be optimal.

As noted, ongoing research underscores the importance of considering both the costs of raising public funds and the benefits of public goods provision, a good example being the "double dividend" debate related to green taxes. If green taxes, non-distortionary by definition, replace distortionary taxes they may lower the MCPF by reducing taxation inefficiencies. Whether or not there exists a double dividend is not clear, in general. We return to this issue in section 5. For a compact summary of the literature on green double dividends, see Jaeger (2024).

Tax evasion by multinationals is another contemporary issue of significant interest. Johansson et al. (2023) study an electricity tax exemption used in Sweden to attract investments in data centers. This exemption tended to benefit multinationals, given the difficulty of taxing their profits. The lost tax revenue, estimated to be in the order of 100 million EUR might have to be replaced by distortionary taxes, potentially increasing the MCPF.

This capsule summary of the history of MCPF barely scratches the surface of the rich literature. For a detailed account of the MCPF concept and its development, a useful place to start is the comprehensive summary by Dahlby (2008).

3 The MCPF under Lump-Sum Taxation

In this section, the basic model used in this Element is introduced. The focus is on the case where lump-sum taxation is available. Mostly, there are distortionary taxes on a good and/or labor, otherwise the MCPF would equal one. A conventional CBA is compared to the Marginal Value of Public Funds and the benefit–cost ratio as a decision criterion. Finally, the SMCPF is introduced and contrasted to the MCPF. A weakness of the concept when applied in a social CBA is highlighted. The reader who wants to read more on CBA is referred to, for example, Boadway and Bruce (1984), Boardman et al. (2018), Brent (2006), de Rus (2021), Florio (2014), Johansson and Kriström (2016, 2018), Just et al. (2004), or Krutilla and Graham (2023). The typical project considered in this Element involves a public good. Most of the books referred to in Section 2 discuss how to value a public good. There are both stated preference and revealed preference methods. The former methods are based on surveys where agents typically are asked about their willingness to pay for, say, an environmental good, such as climate change. The latter methods draw on market prices. For example, if an agent is willing to pay for the gasoline needed to visit a natural park, the willingness to pay for the visit equals at least what is paid for the gasoline.

We do not discuss the optimal size of a government explicitly, although the optimal provision of a public good could be seen as a proxy for the optimal size of a government. A very recent contribution is provided by McCarthy (2024), who discusses the optimal size of a government. According to McCarthy (2024, p. 1), in an open economy debt must have deadweight costs equal to the MCPF, so pure Ricardian equivalence, i.e., the idea that consumers anticipate the future so if they receive a tax cut financed by government borrowing they anticipate future taxes will rise, cannot hold and government bonds must be negative net wealth. In a closed economy, however, these deadweight costs will shut down the possibility of government borrowing entirely, and the optimum size of the public sector returns to the pure modified Samuelson rule in the case of a balanced budget.

3.1 The Basic Model

Often, the MCPF is derived in splendid isolation. Then it is hard to see how to apply the concept in CBA. What cost should be multiplied by an MCPF? Can you simply multiply the considered project's costs by a "multiplier" however defined? The intention here is to provide and discuss the concept in terms of a project. This makes it obvious that the concept of the MCPF is sensitive to the way an evaluator of a project defines the project's costs, for example, at producer or consumer prices. Different concepts sometimes are taken to be identical.

Because distributional issues are out of scope initially, we assume there is a single representative agent. The indirect utility function of the representative agent is very simple to avoid not seeing the wood for the trees. There are just two private goods, one of which serves as the untaxed numéraire; refer to Auerbach and Hines (2002, pp. 1362–65) for a fine discussion of tax normalization. In addition, there is a public good, i.e., a good that benefits or can be consumed by all agents and typically is provided for free through taxation, which is used to generate cost–benefit rules.[2] There is also homogenous labor.

The resulting indirect utility function (assumed to be "well-behaved" in the sense of textbooks on microeconomics), which also serves as the social welfare function, is defined as follows:

$$
\begin{aligned}
V &= V(z, q, w_d, m) \\
&= \max_{x^d, x^{nu}, L^s} U\left(z, x^d, x^{nu}, \mathrm{TE} - L^s\right) \quad \text{s.t.} \quad m + w_d \cdot L^s = q \cdot x^d + 1 \cdot x^{nu},
\end{aligned}
$$

$$(3.1)$$

where z denotes the exogenous supply/provision of the public good, x^d denotes a taxed good, x^{nu} denotes the numéraire whose price is normalized to unity, $q = p + t$ denotes the consumer or end-user price of a commodity, $w_d = w \cdot (1 - t_w)$ denotes the after-tax wage rate, t denotes a unit tax t_w denotes a proportional tax, $m = \pi^x + \pi^{nu} - T = \pi - T$ denotes lump-sum income, π^x and π^{nu} denote profit incomes, T denotes a lump-sum tax, TE denotes the time endowment, and L^s denotes labor supply. Thus, we cover two types of common distortionary taxes and a lump-sum tax. In the general case, the demand functions for the private goods, have the same arguments as the indirect utility function. The same holds for the labor supply, but the arguments are suppressed to simplify notation. Note that one could interpret q and w_d as vectors. Then, the model covers, for example, a value-added tax (VAT) and different marginal income taxes on different types of labor. We will return to this interpretation later on. Subsection A.1 of the Appendix outlines the maximization problem behind the indirect utility function in equation (3.1).

The public sector supplies the public good using labor L^z as the sole input with $L^z = f^{-1}(z)$ if the production function $z = f(L^z)$ is inverted. The sector's budget constraint is written as follows:

$$
T + t \cdot x^d + t_w \cdot w \cdot L^s = w \cdot L^z. \tag{3.2}
$$

Thus, as mentioned in the previous paragraph, there is a unit tax on demand for the private good and a proportional tax on labor supply. Note that at least one tax must be endogenous and adjusted to "balance" the budget, i.e., just like L^z, be a function of z. Any compliance and similar costs discussed in Section 2 are ignored; refer also to the classification of cost items provided by Bos et al. (2019). Equation (3.2) implies that the government's budget is always

---

[2] A measure providing improved outdoor air quality in a region is a simple example of a public good. Everyone can enjoy the improvement, and nobody can be excluded from "consuming" it. It is hard to see how to price an agent's consumption of better air quality. Rather, it is expected to be paid for through some form of taxation.

balanced; there is no surplus or deficit. However, the balance requirement need not imply that all three tax instruments are always available.

We will make two simplifying assumptions, often employed by analysts looking at the MCPF. First, preferences are weakly separable in z and other goods. This means that x^d and L^s, as well as the government's budget, are unaffected by a ceteris paribus change in z (except through L^z), i.e., $x^d = x^d(q, w_d, m)$ and $L^s = L^s(q, w_d, m)$. Weak separability allows us to focus on the MCPF without considering any spending on z but the direct WTP; without this assumption, a typical project also impacts the tax base (in a way that is hard to estimate). This is illuminated in equation (7.6) in Subsection 7.1 and Subsection A.1 in the Appendix. Second, following the tradition within the field, in general, price changes are ignored; refer to Gahvari (2006) for a discussion and justification. Nevertheless, Subsection 5.10 introduces a variation where the price of a commodity is flexible. In contrast, Subsection 5.11 looks at the case where general equilibrium prices are "driven" by the project under evaluation. An endogenous wage rate is considered in Subsection A.5 of the Appendix.

3.2 A Simple Cost–Benefit Rule under Lump-Sum Taxation

In this subsection, the distortionary taxes $t \geq 0$ and $t_w \geq 0$ remain constant. Thus, the lump-sum tax T is the main tax instrument. A simple, nontechnical interpretation of the MCPF when there are no distortionary taxes is as follows. Suppose the lump-sum tax is increased to yield an extra ΔT in tax revenue (but ΔT is assumed to be reasonably small). The agent pays ΔT, and the tax revenue increases by ΔT, i.e., $\Delta T / \Delta T = 1$. The amount ΔT also reflects what the agent at most is willing to pay to avoid the increase in the tax. In any case, the MCPF equals one. Next, suppose there is a tax t on one of the consumption goods. Then, the tax revenue falls short of ΔT by an amount equal to $(t\Delta x^d / \Delta m)\,\Delta T$ because the increase in T (typically) causes demand for x^d to decrease through an income effect, counteracting the tax revenue increase. If there is a proportional tax on labor, there is (typically) a positive effect of ΔT on labor supply. Then, the ratio of the ΔT paid, and the increase in tax revenue equals:

$$\frac{\Delta T}{\Delta T - \left(t\Delta x^d / \Delta m\right)\Delta T - (t_w \cdot w\Delta L^s / \Delta m)\Delta T} = \frac{1}{1 - t\frac{\Delta x^d}{\Delta m} - t_w \cdot w\frac{\Delta L^s}{\Delta m}}$$

$$\approx MCPF^T.$$

This approximates the cost of raising an additional euro in tax revenue. If goods are normal, then $\Delta x^d / \Delta m > 0$ while $\Delta L^s / \Delta m < 0$. If the change in the lump-sum tax is marginal, then the middle expression reduces to MCPF^T in equation (3.4).

To provide a more formal derivation of this result, differentiate equation (3.1) with all prices and distortionary taxes kept constant, to obtain:

$$\frac{dV}{V_m} = \frac{V_z}{V_m}dz - dT, \tag{3.3}$$

where $V_z = \partial V/\partial z$ denotes the marginal utility provided by the public good z, $V_m = \partial V/\partial m$ denotes the marginal utility of lump-sum income m, equal to the Lagrange multiplier associated with the agent's budget constraint, and $(V_z/V_m)\,dz$ captures the marginal WTP for the public good. The increase in T is associated with a negative income effect. However, in itself, this cost–benefit rule is not very helpful.

Using equation (3.2), the change in the lump-sum tax can be expressed as:

$$dT\left(1 - t\frac{\partial x^d}{\partial m} - t_w \cdot w\frac{\partial L^s}{\partial m}\right) = wdL^z \Rightarrow$$

$$dT = wdL^z \cdot \frac{1}{1 - t\frac{\partial x^d}{\partial m} - t_w \cdot w\frac{\partial L^s}{\partial m}} = wdL^z \cdot MCPF^T. \tag{3.4}$$

Recall that $m = \pi - T$ with π kept constant so that $dm = -dT$ in (3.4). Equation (3.4) illuminates what we want to measure. The direct project cost multiplied by $MCPF^T$ equals the government's total expenditure change, i.e., dT. The two final terms of the denominator of $MCPF^T$ capture the income effects on demand for the consumption commodity and the labor supply when disposable income is reduced by a slight increase in the lump-sum tax, given $t, t_w > 0$. It is seen that if there are no distortionary taxes, then $MCPF^T = 1$.

Combining equations (3.3) and (3.4), the following cost–benefit rule is obtained:

$$\frac{dV}{V_m} = \frac{V_z}{V_m}dz - wdL^z \cdot MCPF^T. \tag{3.3'}$$

Thus, the WTP for a small increase in the provision of the public good is compared with the direct or upfront cost of providing the good multiplied by the $MCPF^T$.

Alternatively, one could arrive at equation (3.3) by maximizing (3.1) subject to (3.2). Then, the government is seen as maximizing social welfare subject to its budget constraint. The Lagrangian is as follows:

$$F(.) = V\,(z, q, w_d, m) + \lambda \cdot \left(T + t \cdot x^d\,(.) + t_w \cdot w \cdot L^s\,(.) - w \cdot L^z\right), \tag{3.5}$$

where λ denotes a Lagrange multiplier.

First-order conditions for an interior solution to the decision problem in equation (3.5) are:

$$\frac{\partial F}{\partial T} = -V_m + \lambda \cdot \left(1 - t\frac{\partial x^d}{\partial m} - t_w \cdot w\frac{\partial L^s}{\partial m}\right) = 0$$

$$\frac{\partial F}{\partial z} = V_z - \lambda \cdot w\frac{\partial L^z}{\partial z} = 0$$

$$\frac{\partial F}{\partial \lambda} = T + t \cdot x^d + t_w \cdot w \cdot L^s - w \cdot L^z = 0, \tag{3.6}$$

where $\partial x^d/\partial z = \partial L^s/\partial z = 0$ due to the assumption that preferences are weakly separable in z and other goods. At the second-best optimum, the MCPF is defined as follows:

$$MCPF^T = \frac{\lambda}{V_m} = \frac{1}{\left(1 - t\frac{\partial x^d}{\partial m} - t_w \cdot w\frac{\partial L^s}{\partial m}\right)}. \tag{3.7}$$

This is seen from the first line in equation (3.6).

Multiplying the second line in equation (3.6) by one over V_m converts the expression from units of utility to monetary units. Thus, at a second-best optimum, the CBA reads:

$$\frac{dV}{V_m} = \frac{V_z}{V_m} - \frac{\lambda}{V_m} \cdot w\frac{\partial L^z}{\partial z} = 0. \tag{3.3''}$$

This is the same rule as derived by differentiating the indirect utility function and stated in equation (3.3'), although (3.3'') is evaluated at the second-best optimum, and dz is ignored.

Several observations follow.

- First, if there were no distortionary taxes, i.e., there is an optimal tax system, then the total cost of financing the project equals $dT = wdL^s$ so that $MCPF^T = 1$. Then, equation (3.3'') replicates Samuelson's (1954) rule for the optimal provision of a public good but for a single-agent society.
- Second, with distortionary taxation, whether $MCPF^T$ exceeds or falls short of one is not obvious because if commodities are normal there are counteracting income effects: $\partial x^d/\partial m > 0$ while $\partial L^s/\partial m < 0$ in equation (3.7). Thus, if $t_w = 0$, then $MCPF^T > 1$, while if $t = 0$, then $MCPF^T < 1$.[3] The unit tax typically reduces demand for the taxed good and, hence, undermines the tax base, causing an extra cost. On the other hand, the income tax typically

---

[3] However, even though $MCPF^{t_w} < 1$, the total project cost decreases if one switches to lump-sum taxation. Recall that t_w is distortionary.

induces the agent to work more, hence adding to the tax base, and reducing the total cost of the considered project.

- Third, we have assumed that one of the goods is subject to a unit tax. Shifting to constant ad valorem taxation implies that t is replaced by $t \cdot p$ in the $MCPF^T$'s denominator.
- Fourth, if the project is optimally sized, i.e., such that $dV/V_m = 0$, then the ratio between marginal benefits and direct costs equals the MCPF.[4]
- Fifth, the optimal provision of z is unaffected by the tax normalization rule, i.e., it does not matter whether there is an untaxed numéraire (as assumed here) or t or t_w is set equal to zero. The reason is that the tax normalization rule affects the MCPF and the marginal utility of income symmetrically. This can be seen using the middle line in equation (3.6); see Gahvari (2006, p. 1255) for details.
- Sixth, multiplying the income effects in (A.4) by $(m/x^d) \cdot (x^d/m)$ and $(m/L^s) \cdot (L^s/m)$, respectively, $MCPF^T$ can be interpreted in terms of income elasticities for the demand of the good and the supply of labor. That is, the percentage increase, if normal, in demand for the good (the percentage decrease of the supply of labor) as lump-sum income increases by one percent.

The project is valued at the market wage before tax, i.e., at factor price. Thus, the project displaces production/employment elsewhere valued at w or the value of the marginal product (although the MCPF modifies this outcome). This rule is slightly adjusted if the assumption of weak separability of the public good and other goods is abandoned; refer to Subsection A.1 in the Appendix for details. If the production of z also requires the private good, given weak separability, the same principle applies as for labor, i.e., value at factor price. This issue is addressed in Subsection 5.1.

3.3 Extending the Analysis to Two Other Approaches

We have considered a simple CBA in which the project's upfront cost is multiplied by $MCPF^T$ and deducted from the project's monetary benefits. Next, consider two other ways of empirically assessing the economic benefits and costs of marginally expanding the public good provision. The first one is the benefit–cost ratio, BCR. The other is the Marginal Value of Public Funds,

---

[4] The ratio (and the internal rate of return) may fail to rank projects correctly. However, the ratio works if there is a binding constraint on total expenditures. See Johansson and Kriström (2016, pp. 59–60) for details.

MVPF.[5] Drawing on the second line in equation (3.6), a small project should be undertaken if:

$$\text{CBA:} \quad \frac{dV}{V_m} = WTP^z - wdL^z \cdot MCPF^T = 0,$$

$$\text{BCR:} \quad \frac{dV}{V_m} \frac{1}{wdL^z \cdot MCPF^T} = \frac{WTP^z}{wdL^z \cdot MCPF^T} = 1,$$

$$\text{MVPF:} \quad \frac{dV}{V_m} \frac{1}{wdL^z} = \frac{WTP^z}{wdL^z} - \frac{\lambda}{V_m} = MVPF^z - MCPF^T = 0, \qquad (3.8)$$

where $WTP^z = (V_z/V_m)\, dz$ denotes the willingness to pay for dz, $MCPF^T = \lambda/V_m$, and MVPF of an increase in z equals the WTP for the increase divided by the net cost of the increase. The first line provides a "conventional" CBA, where costs are adjusted by the MCPF. The second line evaluates the ratio of the benefits and total costs of the project.[6] The third line compares the project's WTP per euro of (here only upfront) costs with its MCPF. According to Hendren and Sprung-Keyser (2020, p. 8), "The MVPF of a tax change tells us how much individuals are willing to pay to avoid the tax increase per dollar of net government revenue that is raised." That WTP equals $\lambda/V_m = MCPF^T$ in equation (3.8). For comparisons of the properties of the three criteria in equation (3.8), refer to García and Heckman (2022) and Hendren and Sprung-Keyser (2020, 2022).

Note that converting the utility benefits and costs to monetary units does not affect the sign of the economic evaluation, i.e., all approaches preserve the sign of the change in utility dV. The change in utility is just scaled up or down. Dividing the marginal utility of the public good by the private marginal utility of income (after multiplication by dz) provides the WTP for a small change in the provision of the public good. This concept can be estimated using survey techniques, such as contingent valuation, or travel cost models. Similarly, estimating/approximating the MCPF can be done using economic variables such as income (and price) elasticities; our equation (3.8) can easily be restated to be expressed in terms of income elasticities. Such elasticities can be estimated using, for example, econometric techniques.

3.4 The MCPF versus Diamond's Social MCPF (SMCPF)

In this subsection, the properties of Diamond's (1975) concept, which we, following Lundholm (2005), term the SMCPF, are examined, but note that the

---

[5] The MVPF models used by Hendren and Sprung-Keyser (2020, 2022) account for a broader set of measures than those considered here, but the current approach is sufficient to cover the MVPF concept.

[6] We assume a flexible budget. Spackman (2023) argues in favor of assuming a fixed budget and ranking projects according to their benefit–cost ratios.

term SMCPF is also used to refer to the SMCPF in multi-household economies; see, for example, Bessho and Hayashi (2013). Subsubsection 3.4.1 introduces the concept, showing that an economic evaluation drawing on the SMCPF if correctly undertaken, reduces to a conventional CBA. In Subsubsection 3.4.2, a fundamental problem with the approach as applied by some authors is illuminated. Subsubsection 3.4.3 contains a numerical illustration of the fundamental problem with evaluations based on the SMCPF.

3.4.1 Why the SMCPF Is Superfluous in Economic Evaluations: A Novel Result

The concept examined so far converts utility units to monetary units using the private marginal utility of income. There is an alternative approach that instead uses what is termed the *social* marginal utility of income as the exchange rate between units of utility and monetary units. This variable accounts for income effects on tax bases. The associated marginal cost measure is termed the SMCPF; see, for example, Diamond (1975) and Jacobs (2018); Jacobs seems to be today's leading proponent of the approach.[7]

To arrive at the SMCPF, consider the social marginal utility of lump-sum income, a concept due to Diamond (1975):

$$\kappa = V_m + \lambda \cdot t \frac{\partial x^d}{\partial m} + \lambda \cdot t_w \cdot w \frac{\partial L^s}{\partial m}, \tag{3.9}$$

where the right-hand side equals $\partial F/\partial m = -\partial F/\partial T$. Thus, the Diamond (1975) definition includes the social value of income effects on tax bases. The SMCPF is defined as follows:

$$SMCPF^T = \frac{\lambda}{\kappa}. \tag{3.10}$$

If both x and L are normal, then $\partial x^d/\partial m > 0$ while $\partial L^s/\partial m < 0$ in equations (3.9) and (3.10). Hence, if both t and t_w are strictly positive, then it is unclear whether $SMCPF^T$ exceeds or falls short of $MCPF^T$.

Using (3.9) in the first line of equation (3.6) to eliminate V_m, one finds that at the second-best tax optimum $\kappa = \lambda$. Thus, at this optimum, the SMCPF equals one. We presume that this result explains why some economists recommend using the SMCPF in economic evaluations.

At a second-best tax optimum, the social CBA can be stated as follows:

$$\text{SCBA}: \frac{dV}{\kappa} = WTP^z \cdot \frac{V_m}{\kappa} - wdL^z \cdot 1 = 0. \tag{3.11}$$

---

[7] Refer also to Lundholm (2005) and Holtsmark (2019).

The SCBA approach in equation (3.11) requires that the WTP is adjusted by the ratio of V_m and κ. This might seem impossible in practice, but there are attempts to estimate the marginal utility of income. Refer, for example, to Groom and Maddison (2019), who provide estimates for the UK, and Layard et al. (2008) who found that the marginal utility of income declines somewhat faster than in proportion to the rise in income. Nevertheless, noting that $\kappa = \lambda$ at the second-best optimum so that $V_m/\kappa = V_m/\lambda$ in equation (3.11), and using equation (3.7), monetary benefits in equation (3.11) can be expressed as $WTP^z/MCPF^T$, and the SCBA becomes:

$$\frac{dV}{\kappa} = WTP^z \frac{1}{MCPF^T} - wdL^z. \tag{3.11'}$$

Multiplying through by $MCPF^T = \lambda/V_m$, using the fact that $\lambda = \kappa$, the left-hand side becomes dV/Vm, and the MCPF is shifted to the cost side. Thus, at the second-best optimum, the outcome replicates the one of a conventional CBA. To the best of our knowledge, this is a novel result. In any case, there seems to be no reason to turn to the SMCPF, at least not if the purpose is to undertake a CBA.

3.4.2 Why the Standard Application of the SMCPF Is Problematic: A Novel Result

The SCBA stated in equation (3.11') differs from the definition suggested by Jacobs (2018), who, as mentioned in Section 3.4.1, seems to be today's leading proponent of the SMCPF approach. Refer also to Holtsmark (2019). Bos et al. (2019) argue in favor of the SMCPF being set equal to one but have been strongly criticized by Boardman et al. (2020). According to Jacobs (2018, footnote 28), the Dutch government assumes that SMCPF $= 1$ in its cost–benefit analyses of public sector projects.

Jacobs (2018) calculates the left-hand side expression in the following comparison:

$$WTP^z - wdL^z \cdot 1 = \frac{V_z}{V_m}dz - wdL^z \cdot \frac{\lambda}{\kappa} \genfrac{}{}{0pt}{}{>}{<} \frac{dV}{\kappa} = WTP^z \cdot \frac{1}{MCPF^T} - wdL^z, \tag{3.12}$$

where dV/κ is identical to equation (3.11'), at least one of the distortionary taxes t and t_w is strictly positive but fixed, and $\lambda = \kappa$ at the second-best optimum.[8] The left-hand expression in (3.12) is seemingly a conventional CBA. However, the following expression in (3.12) reveals that this outcome is

---

[8] In Jacobs (2018), see for example, equations (18) and (22), utility benefits are converted using the private marginal utility of income, denoted u_c, while utility costs are converted using the social marginal utility of income, denoted $\alpha(n)$ and defined in equation (11), just as in the second expression in (3.12). The SMCPF, defined in Jacobs's equation (12) with $\alpha(n)$ in the

achieved by converting utility benefits and costs to monetary units using different and unobservable "exchange rates" (V_m and κ, respectively).[9] Thus, the properties of dV/κ are not preserved by the two left-hand side expressions in (3.12), in general. The exception occurs if (and only if) $\kappa = V_m$, i.e., when there are no income effects in equation (3.9), implying that $SMCPF^T = MCPF^T = 1$.[10] If V_m/κ exceeds (falls short of) one, then the two left-hand side expressions in (7) underestimate (overestimate) the social profitability of the considered project, i.e., dV/κ. This assumes that the SMCPF equals one for the nonoptimal z-level suggested by the two left-hand side expressions in equation (3.12). There seems to be no support for this assumption except when the utility function is quasi-linear. This is further illuminated in Subsection 3.4.3.

Hence, the two left-hand side expressions in (3.12) do not replicate a Samuelson (1954) second-best optimal level for the provision of the public good, in general. The exception occurs if $V_m = \kappa$, because then $dV = 0$ at the same z-quantity (optimum) as prescribed by the two left-hand side expressions in (3.12).

3.4.3 A Numerical Illustration of the Results

Next, we provide a simple numerical example illustrating the main point made in the previous subsubsection. Suppose we have the following (logarithmic) Cobb-Douglas type of indirect utility function:

$$V(.) = \ln(z) + \ln\left(\frac{m + \text{TE} \cdot w}{2 \cdot (1 + t)}\right) + \ln\left(\frac{m + \text{TE} \cdot w}{2 \cdot w}\right), \tag{3.13}$$

where the second argument on the right-hand side refers to x^d, with $p = 1$, TE denotes the time endowment, the final argument refers to $\text{TE} - L^s$, i.e., leisure time, and $t_w = 0$.

The Lagrangian is stated as follows:

$$F(.) = V(.) + \lambda \cdot \left(T + t \cdot \left(\frac{m + \text{TE} \cdot w}{2 \cdot (1 + t)}\right) - w \cdot z^2\right). \tag{3.14}$$

Thus, $L^z = z^2$. In what follows, m will be set equal to $-T$, and TE to 24.

---

denominator, equals one on the right-hand side of equations (18) and (22) because the SMCPF is evaluated at the second-best optimum.

[9] The same holds if we consider a private good because $\partial V(.)/\partial q = -V_m \cdot x^d$, i.e., the private marginal utility of income is the relevant exchange rate between units of utility and monetary units.

[10] The utility function must be quasi-linear: $V = v(z, q, w_d) + a \cdot m$, where a is a positive constant. Then $\kappa = V_m = a$, ruling out that, by pure chance, $t\partial x^d/\partial m = -t_w \cdot w\partial L^s/\partial m$ in equation (3.9).

First-order conditions for an interior solution are as follows:

$$\frac{\partial F}{\partial T} = \frac{2}{T - 24 \cdot w} + \lambda \cdot \frac{2 + t}{2 + 2 \cdot t} = 0$$

$$\frac{\partial F}{\partial z} = \frac{1}{V_z} - 2 \cdot \lambda \cdot w \cdot z = 0$$

$$\frac{\partial F}{\partial \lambda} = T + t \cdot \left(\frac{24 \cdot w - T}{2 \cdot (1 + t)} \right) - w \cdot z^2 = 0, \tag{3.15}$$

where we have used the fact that $m = -T$, when the private sector faces constant returns to scale and earns zero profits. Solving this equation system, one finds that: $z = 2 \cdot \sqrt{6/5}$, $T = w \cdot (48 - 72 \cdot t)/(5 \cdot (2 + t))$, and $\lambda = 5/(48 \cdot w)$.

(The same solution is obtained if labor serves as numéraire.) Assuming that the private sector uses labor as the sole input and faces constant returns to scale, the equilibrium wage equals $1/\ell$ when ℓ laborers are required per unit of the good. In what follows, it is assumed that $\ell = 1$. It can be shown that $V_m = 5 \cdot (2 + t)/(96 \cdot (1 + t) \cdot w)$; to obtain this result, evaluate $\partial V/\partial m$ for $m = -T$. Hence, $MCPF^T = \lambda/V_m = 2 \cdot (1 + t)/(2 + t)$, i.e., exceeds one whenever $t > 0$.

Evaluating $\kappa = \partial F(.)/\partial m$, one finds that it equals λ, implying that $SMCPF^T = 1$ at the second-best optimum. Therefore, a SCBA of the kind stated on the left-hand side of (3.12) reads:

$$\frac{1}{z} \cdot \frac{1}{V_m} - 2 \cdot w \cdot z \cdot 1 = \frac{1}{z} \cdot \frac{96 \cdot (1 + t) \cdot w}{5 \cdot (2 + t)} - 2 \cdot w \cdot z = 0. \tag{3.12'}$$

This approach suggests that the second-best optimum occurs at $z^J = 4 \cdot \sqrt{3 \cdot (1 + t)/(5 \cdot (2 + t))}$. It is easily verified that the following holds for this expression:

$$\lim_{t \to 0} z^J = 2 \cdot \sqrt{6/5}. \tag{3.16}$$

Thus, the limit of the expression as t approaches zero equals the second-best solution (which, due to the separability of the utility function, equals the first-best solution, although the utility reaches its maximum for $t = 0$). This can also be seen from equation (3.9), according to which $\kappa = V_m$ for $t = t_w = 0$, implying that a SCBA of the kind stated in the left-hand side of (3.12) coincides with a conventional CBA if there are no distortionary taxes. However, a SCBA of the kind stated in equation (3.12') provides an incorrect answer whenever $t > 0$. In the considered C-D case, it overestimates the optimal z-level whenever $t > 0$, and the overestimation increases in t. In addition, if $t > 0$, then there is no reason to believe that $SMCPF^T = 1$ at the z-level suggested by equation (3.12'). Recall that increasing z beyond the second-best optimum requires additional workers and, hence, additional tax revenue.

These claims can be further illuminated by evaluating equation (3.14) with z fixed at z^J and t fixed at, say, 2, i.e., proceeding as if z^J represents a second-best optimum, given t. Thus, solve the first and final lines of (3.15) with $z = z^J$. This causes utility to decrease from around 6.63 when z is fixed at its second-best optimal level $z = 2 \cdot \sqrt{6/5}$ to around 6.57 when $z = z^J$, and the SMCPF, estimated as λ/V_m, equals 19/14, i.e., is no more equal to one (but is lower than the second-best one). Evaluating (3.12'), but with the SMCPF = 19/14 instead of equal to 1, one finds that a marginal increase in z from $z = z^J$ causes a loss of around 12.75. (Using V_m calculated at the second-best optimum to value monetary benefits, the loss increases to 16.1.) Thus, in the current C-D example, the SMCPF approach, as implemented by Jacobs (2018) and others, overestimates the second-best optimal level of provision of the public good. Moreover, the SMCPF deviates from one at the suggested optimum.

A conventional CBA multiplies the second line in equation (3.15) by $1/V_m$, which leaves the optimal z-level unchanged. The same holds if the equation is multiplied by $1/\kappa$ (and the resulting expression can be converted so that the SCBA equals the CBA, as shown following equation (3.11')).

4 Ramsey Taxation

Lump-sum taxation is not necessarily available or used. Then, we end up in what here is termed a Ramsey world; refer to Ramsey (1927). In this subsection, we consider both a unit tax on a good and proportional income taxation. The MEB is also introduced, and the problem of using the concept in economic evaluations is highlighted.

4.1 A Unit Tax on a Good

Suppose that the commodity tax t is used to balance the government's budget, with $T = t_w = 0$. Then, proceeding as in equations (3.3) and (3.4), one obtains:

$$\frac{dV}{V_m} = \frac{V_z}{V_m}dz - x^d dt = \frac{V_z}{V_m}dz - wdL^z \cdot \frac{1}{\left(1 + \frac{t}{x^d}\frac{\partial x^d}{\partial q}\right)}$$

$$= \frac{V_z}{V_m}dz - wdL^z \cdot MCPF^t, \qquad (4.1)$$

where the marginal utility of income, as usual denoted V_m, equals the Lagrange multiplier associated with the agent's budget constraint in equation (A.3) in the Appendix, and $MCPF^T$ is obtained by differentiating (3.2) with $T = t_w = 0$.[11]

---

[11] $-\left[1 + \left(t/x^d\right) \cdot \left(\partial x^d/\partial q\right)\right] \cdot x^d dt + wdL^z = 0$. Hence, $x^d dt$ in (4.1) can be replaced.

Thus, the sign of the tax elasticity of the taxed commodity in the denominator of the MCPF determines whether $MCPF^T$ exceeds or falls short of unity. For almost all goods (except Veblen and Giffen), the price – and hence the tax – elasticity is negative, implying that the tax increase decreases the tax base. Therefore, one expects that $MCPF^t > 1$ but finite; recall that the tax elasticity is typically a fraction of the price elasticity because t is much smaller than q, the consumer price. Refer to Subsection 5.10 for the case where the producer price also adjusts. Note that (4.1) can be expressed in terms of a price elasticity $1/\left[(1+(t/q)\cdot\varepsilon^d\right]$, where ε^d denotes the price elasticity of demand for the commodity. That is, ε^d reflects the percentage change in demand for the good when its end-user price is increased by one percent.

A graphical illustration is provided in Figure 1. The initial tax is t^1, so the consumer price equals $q^1 = p + t^1$, where the producer price remains constant (and $q^0 = p$). Total tax revenue equals $t^1 \cdot x^1$, where $x^1 = x^{d1} = x^{s1}$ denotes the equilibrium quantity. Next, suppose that the tax is increased to t^2, causing the consumer price to increase to $q^2 = p + t^2$. The tax revenue increases to $t^2 \cdot x^2$. The area in the figure referred to as G captures an increase in tax revenue, while the area referred to as R refers to a contraction in revenue. The net increase in tax revenue equals G – R. Provided the increase in the tax is small, R could also be seen as a (rough) proxy for the value of lost output (where the opportunity

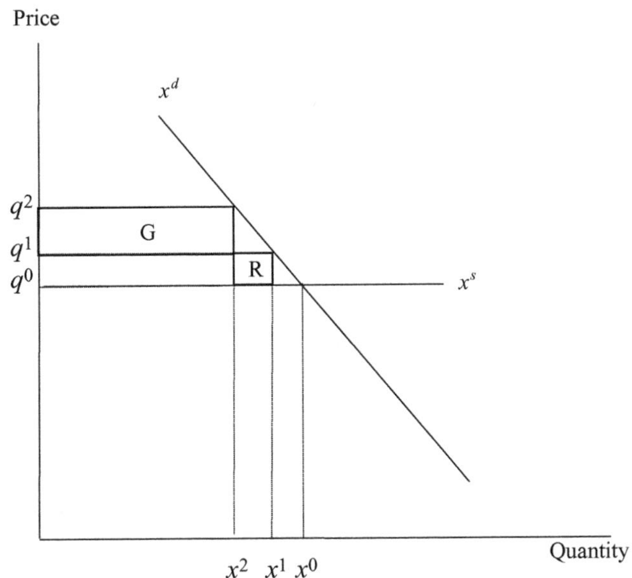

Figure 1 The partial impact of a tax hike

cost per unit equals q^0).[12] This assumption allows a neat simplification of the approximation of the MCPF in equation (4.1').

According to Dahlby (2008, p. 29), one can approximate the MCPF by adding the initial euro paid in tax to obtain:

$$MCPF^t \approx 1 + \frac{R}{G-R} = \frac{G}{G-R}. \tag{4.1'}$$

This measure captures the euro surrendered to the government plus the approximated loss in net output per euro of added tax revenue. For a small increase in the tax, the right-hand side expression could be interpreted as (approximately) the loss of consumer surplus per euro of additional tax revenue. However, it does not make sense to base (non-marginal) welfare evaluations on ordinary or Marshallian demand functions; in general, they do not reflect WTP or the willingness to accept (WTA) compensation. Refer to Figure A.1 in the Appendix for further discussion.

Equation (4.1') goes to 0/0 as the change in the tax goes to zero. Nevertheless, it is possible to relate the approach to equation (4.1) by considering a marginal tax increase from t^1. Then, G shrinks to a line of length x^1. Thus, the tax revenue increases by x^1 (per unit of t); x^1 also reflects a gain in consumer surplus of a marginal decrease in the tax when p remains constant. R reduces to the negative of the tax t^1 times the induced reduction in demand, i.e., to $-t^1 \cdot (\partial x^d / \partial q)$. Thus, this area could also be seen as the marginal increase in the deadweight loss (from the initial triangle). Then, (4.1') is modified to read:

$$MCPF^t = 1 - \frac{t^1 \partial x^d / \partial q}{x^1 + t^1 \partial x^d / \partial q} = \frac{x^1}{x^1 + t^1 \partial x^d / \partial q} = \frac{1}{1 + \frac{t^1}{x^1} \frac{\partial x^d}{\partial q}} \tag{4.1''}$$

This replicates equation (4.1).

The MCPF can also be related to the Laffer curve. Such a curve is illustrated in Figure 2, drawing on a Stone-Geary type of demand function: $x^d = (m-q)/(2 \cdot q)$ with $m = 5$, $q = 1 + t$. The tax revenue equals $t \cdot x^d$, reaching a maximum at $t \approx 1.24$. The slope of the Laffer curve, i.e., the change in tax revenue as t changes, equals the denominator of equation (4.1) multiplied by x^d.[13] $MCPF^t$ equals one for $t = 0$ and goes to infinity – the denominator in (4.1) goes to zero – as one approaches the maximum of the Laffer curve; the slope equals

---

[12] For a small increase in the tax, $R = -t^1 \cdot \Delta x^d$ approximately captures the area under the demand curve between x^1 and x^2 above q^0; compare the marginal measure below. This could be seen as a small expansion of the initial deadweight loss or EB. For a graphical illustration of (a non-marginal) EB, see Figure A.1 in the Appendix.

[13] $d\left(t \cdot x^d\right) / dt = x^d + t \cdot \left(\partial x^d / \partial q\right) = x^d \left(1 + \left(t/x^d\right) \cdot \left(\partial x^d / \partial q\right)\right).$

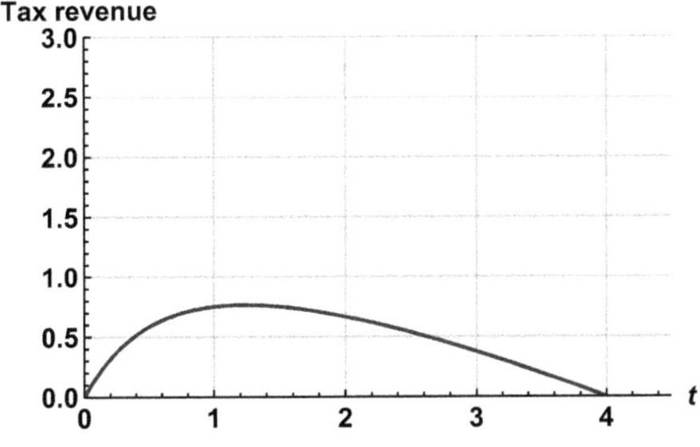

Figure 2 A Laffer curve

zero at the top of the curve. In this case, $MCPF^t$ is undefined to the right of the maximum of the Laffer curve.

However, the Laffer curve need not have a negatively sloped segment. For example, if preferences are Cobb-Douglas, say, $x^d = m/(2 \cdot q)$, tax revenue will approach a maximum as the tax rate (and the $MCPF^t$) go to infinity; commodities are *essential*, implying that the agent cannot "survive" with zero consumption.

4.2 A Proportional Income Tax

Next, assume the project cost is covered by raising the wage tax with $T = t = 0$. Then, the cost–benefit rule equals:

$$\frac{dV}{V_m} = \frac{V_z}{V_m} dz - L^s \cdot w dt_w = \frac{V_z}{V_m} dz - w dL^z \cdot \frac{1}{\left(1 - \frac{t_w \cdot w}{L^s} \frac{\partial L^s}{\partial w_d}\right)}$$

$$= \frac{V_z}{V_m} dz - w dL^z \cdot MCPF^t w. \tag{4.2}$$

In this case, the MCPF is obtained by differentiating (3.2) with $T = t = 0$.[14] The tax elasticity of labor supply determines whether the MCPF exceeds or falls short of unity. If labor supply is increasing in w_d, then the elasticity is positive, and $MCPF^t_w$ exceeds one because the tax increase undermines the tax base. At the same time, $MCPF^t_w$ falls short of one if the increase in the tax rate stimulates labor supply, i.e., if $\partial L^s / \partial w_d < 0$ so that the supply curve for labor is backward-bending and equals one if labor supply is completely inelastic. The $MCPF^t_w$ can also be expressed in terms of the elasticity of labor supply. That is, the percentage change in labor supply as the disposable wage increases by one percent. Simply multiply the tax elasticity in equation (4.2) by w_d/w_d and rearrange terms.

---

[14] $-L^s \cdot w dt_w \left[1 - (t_w \cdot w/L^s) \cdot (\partial L^s/\partial w_d)\right] + w dL^2 = 0$. Hence, $L^s dt_w$ in (4.2) can be replaced.

A Laffer curve with a similar shape as the one depicted in Figure 2 is obtained if labor income is taxed and the supply of labor equals $L^s = (w_d \cdot \text{TE} - 1)/(2 \cdot w_d)$ with $w_d = (1 - t_w) \cdot w$, and a TE equal to 24. Given $t = 0$, tax revenue equals $t_w \cdot w \cdot L^s$ and reaches a maximum at $t_w \approx 0.8$.

In an empirical study, it might be advantageous to base the estimation on the elasticity of taxable income instead. Given a proportional income tax, this concept measures how taxable income changes in response to net-of-tax rate changes, where the net-of-tax rate is one minus the marginal tax rate; refer to, for example, Acheson et al. (2018), Saez (2001), Gruber and Saez (2002), and Saez et al. (2012). In the simple case considered here, if taxable income is denoted $y = w \cdot L^s$, and there is a proportional income tax t_w, then one calculates $\partial y / \partial (1 - t_w)$ to estimate the elasticity. After some calculations, one obtains:

$$MCPF^{t_w} = 1 \Big/ \left(1 - \frac{t_w}{(1 - t_w)} \left[\frac{(1 - t_w)}{y} \frac{\partial y}{\partial (1 - t_w)}\right]\right), \tag{4.3}$$

where the elasticity of taxable income is contained within square brackets.

4.3 A Simple Tax Reform

Let us consider a simple tax reform where holding z constant, the income tax is increased, and the commodity tax is reduced:

$$\frac{dV}{V_m} = -x^d dt - L^s \cdot w dt_w, \tag{4.4}$$

where $dt < 0$ and $dt_w > 0$. The tax reform is such that the total tax revenue remains unchanged. Based on equation (3.2), after some calculations, one obtains:

$$x^d dt \left(1 + \frac{t}{x^d} \frac{\partial x^d}{\partial q} + \frac{t_w \cdot w}{x^d} \frac{\partial L^s}{\partial q}\right) + L^s \cdot w dt_w \left(1 - \frac{t_w \cdot w}{L^s} \frac{\partial L^s}{\partial w_d} - \frac{t}{L^s} \frac{\partial x^d}{\partial w_d}\right) = 0. \tag{4.5}$$

Thus:

$$-x^d dt \frac{MCPF^{t_w}}{MCPF^t} = L^s \cdot w dt_w. \tag{4.6}$$

Hence, using (4.6) in (4.4), the tax reform has the following impact on monetary welfare:

$$\frac{dV}{V_m} = -x^d dt \left(1 - \frac{MCPF^{t_w}}{MCPF^t}\right). \tag{4.7}$$

The tax reform, with $dt < 0$ and $dt_w > 0$, is welfare-improving if $MCPF^t > MCPF^{t_w}$. At the second-best optimum, the marginal cost of raising funds is the same for the two considered taxes, i.e., welfare cannot be increased by marginally shifting from one tax to the other, as seen from (4.7). However, the direct cost of a project must still be multiplied by an MCPF as long as there are distortionary taxes, and the benefit side must be added.

4.4 The MCPF versus the MEB

According to Ballard and Fullerton (1992), one can speak of a Dasgupta-Stiglitz-Atkinson-Stern tradition or MCPF-tradition in which MCPF may be larger or smaller than one and of a Harberger-Pigou-Browning tradition or an MEB tradition in which the MCPF is always larger than unity (a claim that can be challenged, for example, if the tax is addressing a negative externality or if an increase in a labor tax increases labor supply). Dahlby (2008, pp. 42–47) provides a good historical survey of alternative approaches.

The EB is typically defined for discrete tax changes, see, for example, Fullerton (1991), but here we initially focus on the marginal case. Let us use the wage tax as an example. Initially, $V = V(z, p, w \cdot (1 - t_w), m + EV)$ with equivalent variation, $EV = 0$. Then, we look at a marginal EV such that:

$$V_m dEV = V_m \cdot L^S \cdot w dt_w, \tag{4.8}$$

where the marginal equivalent variation dEV is the maximal sum of money the agent is willing to pay to avoid the increase in the labor tax, with $T = t = 0$; refer to Subsection 5.6 for more on income-compensated or Hicksian WTP/WTA measures. The impact of the proposed tax increase on the government's budget when $t = T = 0$ equals:

$$dS^{t_w} = L^S \cdot w dt_w - t_w \frac{\partial L^s}{\partial w_d} w dt_w = \left(1 - \frac{t_w \cdot w}{L^S} \frac{\partial L^s}{\partial w_d}\right) \cdot L^S \cdot w dt_w, \tag{4.9}$$

where S denotes the net surplus of the government's budget, with $T = t = 0$. Combining equations (4.8) and (4.9) yields:

$$\frac{dEV}{dS^{t_w}} = \frac{1}{1 - \frac{t_w \cdot w}{L^S} \frac{\partial L^s}{\partial w_d}} = MCPF^{t_w}. \tag{4.10}$$

Thus, dEV/dS^{t_w} equals the MCPF caused by a marginal tax increase. However, the MEB is obtained by deducting $dS^{t_w}/dS^{t_w} = 1$ from dEV/dS^{t_w} i.e., $MEB^{t_w} = dEV/dS^{t_w} - 1$. This is done to get the change in EB. Dividing dEV by the change in tax revenue dS^{t_w} yields the EB per euro of additional tax revenue. Thus, $MCPF^{t_w} = MEB^{t_w} + 1$.

Drawing instead on the concept of the equivalent surplus, labor supply is kept constant. Then, (4.10) reveals that $MCPF^{t_w}$ equals unity while MEB^{t_w} equals zero. This is so because the tax increase has no impact on labor supply, i.e., $\partial L^s/\partial w_d = 0$ in (4.10).

One can also define the MEB for a commodity. The marginal EV now equals:

$$dEV^t = x^d dt. \tag{4.8'}$$

The surplus is changed as follows:

$$dS^t = \left(1 + \frac{t}{x^d}\frac{\partial x^d}{\partial q}\right) x^d dt. \tag{4.9'}$$

Hence:

$$\frac{dEV^t}{dS^t} = \frac{1}{\left(1 + \frac{t}{x^d}\frac{\partial x^d}{\partial q}\right)} = MCPF^t. \tag{4.10'}$$

This replicates (4.1). Holding demand constant, i.e., turning to an equivalent surplus, the expression equals one because $\partial x^d/\partial q = 0$.

One could also consider a discrete change in the income (or the commodity) tax and evaluate EV/S. However, evaluating EV/S for $t_w^1 \rightarrow t_w^2$ (or $t^1 \rightarrow t^2$) results in $0/0$ because both EV and S go to zero as the tax change goes to zero. (This is why, for example, Auriol and Warlters (2012, p. 61) add one-ten-thousandth of a percentage point to the existing tax rate.) However, in the second step, we differentiate EV and S^{tw} with respect to t_w^1 to obtain dEV and dS^{tw}. In the final step, we evaluate dEV/dS^{tw} for $t_w^1 \rightarrow t_w^2$, i.e., employ l'Hôpital's rule. Using this approach, one can replicate (4.10) and (4.10'). For more on l'Hôpital's rule, see, for example, page 481 in Varian (1992) or Section 8.8.3 in Johansson and Kriström (2016). A numerical illustration is found in Subsection A.2 of the Appendix, which also provides a graphical illustration of the EB.

It seems to be a standard in the CGE literature to estimate EV/S for a small tax increase and interpret it as a measure of the MCPF; see, for example, Auriol and Warlters (2012, p. 58), Barrios et al. (2013, p. 10) or Vásquez Cordano and Balistreri (2010, p. 259). Nevertheless, except in the marginal case, EB + 1 and MCPF are two different concepts addressing different issues; see, for example, Auerbach and Hines (2002, p. 1386). Hence, EV/S is not applicable when evaluating non-marginal projects welfare effects. That said, CGE is a potent tool for evaluating the social benefits and costs of large projects.

5 A Smörgåsbord of Further Topics in Variations of the Basic Model

The MCPF is typically defined "in splendid isolation" as a tax reform or related to a project involving a public good. In this section, we go beyond this practice and examine how a number of factors affect a CBA and the MCPF in variations of the basic model introduced in Sections 3 and 4. A few more technical issues are placed at the end of the section.

5.1 A Produced and Taxed Input

Let us assume that the production of the public good also requires the taxed private good as an input. Moreover, the input is taxed at the same rate as consumption. Then, the government's budget constraint is modified to read:

$$T = w \cdot L^z + q \cdot x^z - t \cdot \left(x^d + x^z \right) - t_w \cdot w \cdot L^s = w \cdot L^z + p \cdot x^z - t \cdot x^d - t_w \cdot w \cdot L^s, \quad (5.1)$$

where $T \geq 0$, and x^z denotes the government's demand for the private good. Thus, what the government pays to itself in the form of taxes vanishes from the constraint. Hence, the input is valued at factor price. The modified cost–benefit rule reads:

$$\frac{dV}{V_m} = \frac{V_z}{V_m} dz - (wdL^z + pdx^z) \cdot MCPF^T. \quad (5.2)$$

Thus, the definition of the MCPF remains unchanged by introducing a taxed input. This fact explains why the project under evaluation in this Element mainly uses labor as the sole input.

However, once both inputs have been introduced, let us point to another way of approximating the total project cost. Suppose that the supply of the produced input is infinitely elastic. Then, $dx^d = 0$ in the differentiated version of equation (5.1), and dx^z is valued at factor price. If the supply is completely inelastic, then private consumption, valued at q per unit, is displaced, i.e., $-dx^d = dx^z$. Hence, p in equation (5.2) is replaced by q (also in the case where the input is untaxed so that $p \cdot x^z$ appears in equation (5.2)). Similarly, if the supply of labor is infinitely elastic, value labor at the after-tax wage because only leisure time is displaced, while if labor supply is entirely inelastic, value at w; in the latter case, production elsewhere is displaced and the value of the marginal product equals the wage. This approach provides reasonable lower and upper bounds for the total project cost without involving any explicit MCPF.

5.2 Revenues Collected by the Project

Suppose there is a user charge on z. We could interpret z either as a public good or as a rationed private good. The good provides utility, just as before, but there is also a payment for each unit of the good. Therefore, the indirect utility function is now written:

$$V = V(z, q, w_d, \pi - p^z \cdot z), \quad (5.3)$$

where p^z denotes the price per unit of z, and any sign denoting a constraint on the consumption of z is suppressed; refer to Cuddington et al. (1984) and Johansson and Kriström (2016, Section 3.7) for this kind of function; maximize utility subject to the budget constraint and a constraint on the consumption of z to obtain the indirect utility function. Sticking to a Ramsey world, the government's budget constraint now reads:

$$t \cdot x^d + t_w \cdot L^s + p^z \cdot z - w \cdot L^z = 0. \tag{5.4}$$

Thus, pricing z reduces the need for tax hikes. Suppose, for simplicity, that t is adjusted to balance the budget with $t_w = 0$. Then, the project evaluation rule reads:

$$\frac{dV}{V_m} = \frac{V_z}{V_m} dz - x^d dt - p^z dz. \tag{5.5}$$

Using the government's budget constraint, one arrives, after some calculations, at the following project appraisal rule:

$$\frac{dV}{V_m} = \frac{V_z}{V_m} dz - p^z dz - \left(w dL^z - p^z dz + t \frac{\partial x^d}{\partial m} p^z dz \right) \cdot \frac{1}{1 + \frac{t}{x^d} \frac{\partial x^d}{\partial q}}, \tag{5.6}$$

where now $m = \pi - p^z \cdot z$. Thus, it is hardly surprising that the revenue obtained from supplying dz is deducted from the cost of providing the extra units before multiplying by the multiplier. Also note that if z is priced such that the marginal WTP for z equals p^z, i.e., the ration just "bites," then the two first terms on the right-hand side of (5.6) sum to zero. However, setting $w dL^z - p^z dz = 0$, i.e., $MC^z = p^z$ in the expression within parentheses, where p^z can be interpreted as a Lindahl price in the considered single-agent society, does not represent a first-order condition for an interior optimum in this second-best world; there is a "deadweight" impact through the income argument in equation (5.3) as z is changed and reflected by the final term within parentheses in (5.6).[15] Recall that the increase in z causes the agent to pay more for z, reducing the tax base. If the public sector earns a surplus, it is magnified if the multiplier $MCPF^t$ exceeds one because the distortive tax can be reduced.

5.3　A Tax on Emissions

In this subsection, the considered project is financed by increasing a tax on emissions of a damaging gas or particle caused by the considered private good (but emissions caused by the project are considered later on). This is the limited

---

[15] Even though the utility function is assumed to be weakly separable in z and other goods, x^d is affected by $p_z \cdot z$ through the income argument. On Lindahl prices, see, for example, Lindahl (1958) or section 2.4 of Laffont (1988).

purpose, implying that we do not consider a green tax shift, also known as environmental fiscal reform. The indirect utility function is now assumed to be as follows:

$$V = V(z, q, w_d, m, Em),$$

(5.7)

where $q = p + t + t_{Em}, t_{Em}$ denotes a tax introduced to combat emissions, and $Em = R + g(x^d)$ denotes damages, here as a function of emissions from the rest of the world R, taken to be given, and from the private good; compare car driving and emissions of CO_2. To simplify the discussion, preferences are assumed to be weakly separable in z and Em and other goods. The government's budget constraint is taken to be:

$$(t + t_{Em}) \cdot x^d - w \cdot L^z = 0.$$

(5.8)

The green tax t_{Em} is used to finance a small increase in z. (For example, Sweden has a CO_2 tax, an energy tax and VAT on gasoline, but please do not ask what the difference is between an energy and a CO_2 tax!)

Proceeding as previously, in the first step, one arrives at the following evaluation rule:

$$\frac{dV}{V_m} = \frac{V_z}{V_m}dz - x^d dt_{Em} + \frac{V_{Em}}{V_m}g_x\frac{\partial x^d}{\partial q}dt_{Em} = \frac{V_z}{V_m}dz - x^d dt_{Em}\left(1 - \frac{V_{Em}}{V_m}g_x\frac{1}{x^d}\frac{\partial x^d}{\partial q}\right),$$

(5.9)

where g_x denotes the marginal damage, and $V_{Em}/V_m < 0$ denotes the marginal disutility caused by a small increase in emissions converted to monetary units by division by V_m (where V_m treats emissions as exogenous). The final term in the middle equality of (5.9) could be interpreted as the negative of the marginal WTP for fewer damages times the (usually negative) change in damages as the tax increases. Hence, the term is usually positive.

Differentiating (5.8) with $dt = 0$ and using it in (5.9), one obtains, after some calculations, the following evaluation rule:

$$\frac{dV}{V_m} = \frac{V_z}{V_m}dz - wdL^z\left(1 - \frac{V_{Em}}{V_m}g_x\frac{1}{x^d}\frac{\partial x^d}{\partial q}\right)\frac{1}{1 + \frac{(t+t_{En})}{x^d}\frac{\partial x^d}{\partial q}}.$$

(5.10)

Provided x^d is a normal good, the project now earns an additional benefit, as covered by the final term within parentheses in the numerator of the equation. Provided a tax increase reduces demand for the taxed good, the project is attributed the marginal WTP for reduced damages times a factor capturing the reduction in damages; recall that $V_{Em} < 0$. This gain is scaled up (or exceptionally scaled down) by the multiplier. It cannot be ruled out that the total MCPF is smaller than one, even when the multiplier exceeds one.

Next, suppose that the considered project adds to emissions. If it pays the tax t_{Em} for its emissions, the cost is, at the same time, an income for the government, hence it vanishes from the government's budget constraint. Therefore, (5.10) is simply augmented by the term $(V_{Em}/V_m)\,g_z^z dz$, where g_z^z denotes the marginal damage caused by z. Thus, the project causes societal costs through its polluting activities. This case is further illuminated in Subsection A.3 of the Appendix, including a simple numerical illustration that results in a total MCPF below one. Thus, this case illuminates the dangers of applying "standardized" measures of the MCPF in empirical evaluations of projects and policies.

If the project must acquire permits to cover its emissions of greenhouse gases, the entire cost of the permits is added to the wage cost and multiplied by the relevant multiplier, for example, the one in equation (4.1). Given a fixed number of permits, the project simply displaces other activities that require permits. Equivalently, the government loses revenue because it can no longer sell the permits to other agents. Refer to the discussion in Jorge-Calderón and Johansson (2017) and Johansson (2020) and, for example, Rosendahl (2019) for a discussion of the properties of the reformed EU ETS. The project could also impact on emissions by agents not covered by the permit scheme. In the simple model used here, this would occur through the tax increase necessary to fund the project; compare equations (5.9) and (5.10).

Sometimes a project causes emissions in "the rest of the world," for example, by importing emitting inputs. In such cases, one could add a term reflecting the marginal monetary disutility of emissions multiplied by the quantity of emissions caused elsewhere by the project. This would reflect a kind of altruism because the agent cares about the damage caused to others by her home country's activities. See also Subsection 5.9. For more on externalities, refer to Kaplow (2008).

5.4 A Profit Tax

Thus far, taxes have been paid by the agent through taxes on demand for goods or supply of labor. Therefore, let us examine how a profit tax works. The indirect utility function is written as:

$$V = V(z, q, w_d, m), \tag{5.11}$$

where $m = \pi_d = (1 - t_\pi) \cdot \pi$, and t_π denotes a proportional tax on profit income. Suppose that also consumption of the good is taxed, just as before. The government's budget constraint now reads:

$$t \cdot x^d + t_\pi \cdot \pi - w \cdot L^z = 0. \tag{5.12}$$

Suppose that the profit tax is adjusted to balance (5.12) as the production of the public good is increased, while t is kept constant. The change in monetary welfare equals:

$$\frac{dV}{V_m} = \frac{V_z}{V_m} dz - \pi dt_\pi, \tag{5.13}$$

where changes in prices (and hence in π) are suppressed. Then, from equation (5.12), we have:

$$\pi dt_\pi = wdL^z \frac{1}{1 - \frac{t}{\pi} \frac{\partial x^d}{\partial \pi_d}}, \tag{5.14}$$

where the "demand elasticity with respect to profit income" is most likely positive; $\partial x^d / \partial \pi_d = \partial x^d / \partial m$ denotes an income effect. Hence, one expects the MCPF to exceed unity in this case. The cost–benefit rule reads:

$$\frac{dV}{V_m} = \frac{V_z}{V_m} dz - wdL^z \frac{1}{1 - \frac{t}{\pi} \frac{\partial x^d}{\partial \pi_d}}. \tag{5.15}$$

If initially $t = 0$, then MCPF $= 1$ in this small project case.

5.5 A Project Run by the Private Sector

Often, it is assumed that private sector projects/investments display other investments. Therefore, it is claimed that there is no MCPF. Nevertheless, let us briefly examine whether there is an MCPF also if the private sector undertakes a (extremely stylized) project. In so doing, assume that a second firm produces the taxed private good. Therefore, in a Ramsey world, the indirect function now reads:

$$V = V(z, q, w_d, m), \tag{5.16}$$

where $m = \pi + \pi^N$, and π^N denotes the profit income earned by the "new" firm. The new firm plans to marginally expand its level of production.

The government's budget constraint is the same as before:

$$t \cdot x^d + t_w \cdot L^s - w \cdot L^z = 0. \tag{5.17}$$

A simple cost–benefit rule, with $t_w = 0$ and suppressing price changes, reads

$$\frac{dV}{V_m} = -x^d dt + pdx^N - wdL^N, \tag{5.18}$$

where $pdx^N - wdL^N = d\pi^N$. Recall that at least one tax rate must be adjusted to balance the government's budget. Use the government's budget constraint to obtain:

$$x^d dt \left(1 + \frac{t}{x^d} \frac{\partial x^d}{\partial q}\right) = -t \frac{\partial x^d}{\partial m} dm, \tag{5.19}$$

where $dm = pdx^N - wdL^N$. Thus, we arrive at the following evaluation rule:

$$\frac{dV}{V_m} = dx^N \left(p - w\frac{dL^N}{dx^N} \right) \cdot \left(1 + t\frac{\partial x^d}{\partial m} \frac{1}{1 + \frac{t}{x^d}\frac{\partial x^d}{\partial q}} \right), \tag{5.20}$$

where $w \cdot (dL^N / dx^N)$ denotes the marginal cost. In the special case under consideration, the addition is valued at producer price (because implicitly, demand increases by dx^N units). In any case, the MCPF is positive and magnifies the social surplus/deficit. However, interpreted this way, the profit-maximizing optimum also represents the social optimum; recall that the price equals the marginal cost at the profit maximum. The same result is obtained by considering a constrained utility maximization problem, as is done in Subsection A.4 of the Appendix. Thus, within this simple model and if optimally scaled, the private sector project should not cause any "extra" welfare cost or benefit to society. Thus, if a public sector project displaces the considered private sector firm, it seems reasonable to set the MCPF equal to one.

5.6 Compensated Equilibrium

The conventional general equilibrium approach draws on Marshallian or uncompensated household demand and supply functions. This approach is used in this Element with the exemption of this brief subsection. One can define a compensated equilibrium by replacing the Marshallian functions with their Hicksian or compensated functions (Debreu, 1959, Arrow and Hahn, 1971).

The expenditure function is defined as follows for our simple standard problem:

$$e\left(z, q, w_d, \overline{U}\right) = \min_{x, x^{nu}, L} \left\{ \left[q \cdot x + 1 \cdot x^{nu} \right.\right.$$
$$\left.\left. + w_d \cdot (\text{TE} - L) \right] \mid U(z, x, x^{nu}, \text{TE} - L) \geq \overline{U} \right\}, \tag{5.21}$$

where $\overline{U}$ denotes the target utility, here taken to be the initial or pre-project level, and z is kept constant.[16] The expenditure function gives the minimum amount of money the agent must spend on goods and leisure, where the price of leisure equals the disposable wage, to achieve at least the target utility. The resulting demand and supply functions are termed Hicksian or compensated functions. The augmented expenditure function is defined as $E(.) = e(.) - m$. The sign convention used is such that the compensating variation, CV, is such that compensating variation, $CV = m^1 - m^0 + e^0(.) - e^1(.)$, where a superscript 0 (1) denotes the expenditure level without (with) a project, and CV denotes a

---

[16] The Lagrangian is $F(.) = q \cdot x + 1 \cdot x^{nu} + w_d \cdot (\text{TE} - L) - v^I \cdot [U(.) - \overline{U}]$.

WTP or a WTA depending on the sign of the expression. Thus, *CV* is positive if lump-sum income increases or if expenditure is reduced. Reverse the sign convention to obtain *EV*. Hence, for a marginal change from the final level $dCV = -dEV$, i.e., when *dCV* is the maximal payment to obtain the change, then *dEV* is the minimal compensation to avoid the change, and vice versa.

Consider now a marginal increase in the provision of the public good financed by lump-sum taxation with t, $t_w > 0$ but kept fixed. The marginal WTP equals $-\left(\partial e^1(.)/\partial z\right) dz = -e^1 dz > 0$ because more of the public good reduces what has to be spent on private goods to maintain the target utility. Drawing on the definition of *CV* provided above, the CBA can be stated as follows:

$$dCV = dm^1 - e_z^1 dz = -dT - e_z^1 dz = -wdL^z - e_z^1 dz, \tag{5.22}$$

where *dCV* denotes the marginal CV that holds the agent at her initial level of utility. The MCPF equals one if the analysis is based on the concept of compensated equilibrium. The simple reason is that there are no income effects, which is in sharp contrast to equation (3.4).

If lump-sum taxation is ruled out, the results resemble those obtained in Subsections 4.1 and 4.2. The main difference is that in the Hicksian case, price changes are associated with substitution effects but no income effects. Therefore, no further analysis of the MCPF based on compensated equilibrium is undertaken in this Element.

5.7 Social Security Fees

In many countries, employers have to pay social security taxes for their employees.[17] Here, it is assumed that employers pay a fraction θ of wages to cover pensions, paid sick leaves, and so on. Thus, the total labor cost "per hour" equals $w\cdot(1 + \theta)$. The government or some other authority collects the tax and returns the tax revenue as a lump-sum payment to the representative agent. Denote the indirect utility function:

$$V\left(z, q, w_d, \pi - w \cdot \theta \cdot L^d + P^G\right), \tag{5.23}$$

where $P^G = \theta \cdot w \cdot \left(L^d + L^z\right)$ denotes the lump sum received to cover pensions, and so on, and the private sector's costs in the profit functions in (5.23) must be augmented by $w \cdot \theta \cdot L^d$ (suppressing, as usual, the numéraire firm). Hence, the net amount received by the single agent owning the private firms equals $P = \theta \cdot w \cdot L^z$.

---

[17] See, for example, https://blog.eurodev.com/social-security-tax-rates-employers-europe-2021.

Ruling out lump-sum taxes, the government's budget constraint is written as:

$$w \cdot (1 + \theta) \cdot L^z = t \cdot x^d + t_w \cdot L^s. \tag{5.24}$$

Suppose that the unit tax on consumption is used to balance the government's budget, with all prices constant and $t_w = 0$. In this case, the evaluation rule can be stated as follows:

$$\frac{dV}{V_m} = \frac{V_z}{V_m} dz - x^d dt + dP. \tag{5.25}$$

Differentiating the government's budget constraint yields:

$$w \cdot (1 + \theta) dL^z = x^d dt + t \cdot \frac{\partial x^d}{\partial q} dt + t \cdot \frac{\partial x^d}{\partial m} dP, \tag{5.26}$$

where $m = \pi + P$, $dP = w \cdot \theta dL^z$ and the final term on the right-hand side is due to an income effect. Equation (5.26) can be restated to read:

$$x^d dt = \left[w \cdot (1 + \theta) dL^z - t \frac{\partial x^d}{\partial m} dP \right] \cdot \frac{1}{1 + \frac{t}{x^d} \frac{\partial x^d}{\partial q}}. \tag{5.27}$$

Using this expression in equation (5.25), the cost–benefit rule can be stated as follows:

$$\frac{dV}{V_m} = \frac{V_z}{V_m} dz - \left[w \cdot (1 + \theta) dL^z - t \cdot \frac{\partial x^d}{\partial m} \cdot w \cdot \theta dL^z \right] \cdot \frac{1}{1 + \frac{t}{x^d} \frac{\partial x^d}{\partial q}} + w \cdot \theta dL^z. \tag{5.28}$$

dP has a positive impact on tax bases, provided the income effect is positive. This reduces the upfront cost of the considered project. There is also the positive final term. If the multiplier equals one, the final term in (5.28) and the public sector's extra expenditure on social security fees sum to zero. However, these two terms combined have a negative impact on welfare if the multiplier exceeds one, but there is a magnified positive impact on tax bases, in general.

The lesson learned from this simple exercise is that social security taxes need not change the formal structure of the "multiplier," although the magnitude of the MCPF is most likely affected.

5.8 Unemployment

In this subsection, we briefly examine if unemployment affects the magnitude of the MCPF. Therefore, we ignore the impact of unemployment on physical and mental well-being, human capital, life expectancy, and so on; refer to Johansson and Kriström (2020) for discussion and further references.

Let us assume that there is an unemployment insurance. For every hour at work, the agent pays a charge γ that entitles her to w_u per hour of involuntary unemployment (or underemployment):

$$\gamma \cdot \bar{L} = w_u \cdot \left(L^s - \bar{L}\right) \tag{5.29}$$

where $\bar{L}$ denotes employment, and the "notional" supply of labor $L^s > \bar{L}$ if unemployment (or perhaps more appropriately underemployment) prevails, here due to a sticky and too high wage rate. The indirect utility function is modified to read as follows:

$$V = V\left(z, q, \pi + (w \cdot (1 - t_w) - \gamma) \cdot \bar{L} + w_u \cdot \left(L^s - \bar{L}\right), \text{TE} - \bar{L}\right). \tag{5.30}$$

Equation (5.30) is obtained by maximizing utility subject to the budget and employment constraints. Due to the employment constraint, there is no wage argument in (5.30), but an argument covering what, from the point of view of the agent, is disposable *lump-sum* income. The (marginal) disutility of work effort is covered by the final argument of the function:

$$(\partial V / \partial \bar{L}) = (\partial V / \partial \ell)(\partial \ell / \partial \bar{L}) = (V_\ell)(-1) = -V_\ell,$$

where ℓ refers to leisure time, V_ℓ denotes the marginal utility of leisure time, and lump-sum income is kept constant. The government's budget constraint is modified to read:

$$t \cdot x^d + t_w \cdot w \cdot \bar{L} - w \cdot L^z = 0. \tag{5.31}$$

First, assume that $t = 0$. Then, using the income tax to finance the change in z and differentiating the indirect utility function yields:

$$\begin{aligned}
\frac{dV}{V_m} &= \frac{V_z}{V_m}dz - \bar{L} \cdot w dt_w + w \cdot (1 - t_w)\, d\bar{L} - \gamma d\bar{L} - \bar{L}d\gamma - w_u d\bar{L} - \frac{V_\ell}{V_m}d\bar{L} \\
&= \frac{V_z}{V_m}dz - \bar{L} \cdot w dt_w + w \cdot (1 - t_w)\, d\bar{L} - \frac{V_\ell}{V_m}d\bar{L},
\end{aligned} \tag{5.32}$$

where it is assumed that $\gamma d\bar{L} + \bar{L}d\gamma + w_u d\bar{L} = 0$, i.e., that the unemployment insurance just breaks even when employment changes marginally, and any change of the "notional" labor supply L^s has been suppressed. The final term on the right-hand side of (5.32) reflects the marginal disutility of work effort converted to monetary units by division by the marginal utility of income.

Moreover, increasing the wage tax in equation (5.31) results in $\bar{L} \cdot w dt_w = w dL^z$ because changing the wage tax has no impact on employment. Therefore, one arrives at the following project appraisal rule:

$$\frac{dV}{V_m} = \frac{V_z}{V_m}dz - w dL^z + \left[w \cdot (1 - t_w) - \frac{V_\ell}{V_m}\right] d\bar{L}. \tag{5.33}$$

If the employment constraint just "bites," then $-V_\ell/V_m = w \cdot (1 - t_w)$, i.e., we are back to a kind of full employment rule. Because employment is fixed, $\partial \bar{L}/\partial t_w = 0$ explaining why the MCPF equals one. If unemployment prevails, there is an additional benefit if the project reduces unemployment because then $w \cdot (1 - t_w) - V_\ell/V_m > 0$, i.e., the absolute value of the marginal disutility of work effort, converted to monetary units, falls short of the after-tax wage. If $d\bar{L} = dL^z$, then the project cost reduces to $[-t_w \cdot w - V_\ell/V_m]\, dL^z$. This adds the tax to the monetary value of the marginal disutility of work effort, i.e., if the employment constraint just bites so that $V_\ell/V_m = w \cdot (1 - t_w)$, then the project cost equals $w \cdot dL^z$

Next, assume that t is used to balance the government's budget with $t_w = 0$ in equations (5.30) and (5.31) . In this case, $x^d = x^d(q, m)$; m is defined following equation (5.34), and z and ℓ are not arguments due to the assumption that preferences are weakly separable in z and ℓ and other goods. After some calculations, the following rule is obtained:

$$\frac{dV}{V_m} = \frac{V_z}{V_m} dz - \left(w dL^z - t \cdot \frac{\partial x^d}{\partial m} \cdot w d\bar{L} \right) \frac{1}{1 + \frac{t}{x^d}\frac{\partial x^d}{\partial q}} + \left[w - \frac{V_\ell}{V_m} \right] d\bar{L}, \quad (5.34)$$

where now $m = (w - \gamma) \cdot \bar{L} + w_u \cdot \left(L^s - \bar{L} \right)$, suppressing any profit income, and the unemployment insurance is assumed to break even when unemployment changes marginally. Thus, in this case, the by-now-familiar multiplier appears in the expression. In addition, if the project reduces unemployment, there is an additional benefit magnified by the multiplier; recall that $\partial x^d/\partial m$ denotes an income effect, which here is taken to be positive. If the economy is close to full employment, the final two terms within square brackets in (5.34) sum to zero; the wage just covers the marginal disutility of work effort. If the MCPF equals one (with $t = 0$) and $d\bar{L} = dL^z$, then value the project's employees at the marginal disutility of work effort converted to monetary units by division by V_m.

In sum, given the simple model applied here, the "multiplier," either vanishes or is left unchanged, depending on how the public sector raises its funds. Thus, tax normalization matters in this case.

5.9 A Tariff on Imports

In principle, a tariff on imports could finance a project. Therefore, it is worthwhile to consider this case briefly. Suppose that we add an imported good, denoted x^M. The economy is assumed to be small, so world market prices are independent of activities in the considered economy. Initially, we also assume that the project we evaluate is so small that the exchange rate remains constant.

The indirect utility function is now stated as follows:

$$V = V\left(z, q, q^M, w_d, m\right), \tag{5.35}$$

where a superscript M denotes the imported good, $q^M = 1 + t^M$ if the world market price is equal to unity, and t^M is a unit tariff on imports.

The government's budget constraint is now equal to:

$$t \cdot x^d + t^M \cdot x^M + t_w \cdot w \cdot L^s - w \cdot L^z = 0, \tag{5.36}$$

ruling out lump-sum taxation. Next, suppose a small increase in the provision of the public good is financed by raising the tariff. Then, proceeding as in previous subsections, we arrive at the following initial evaluation rule:

$$\frac{dV}{V_m} = \frac{V_z}{V_m} dz - x^M dt^M. \tag{5.37}$$

Differentiating (5.36) and eliminating the tax expression from (5.37), one obtains the following evaluation rule:

$$\frac{dV}{V_m} = \frac{V_z}{V_m} dz - \frac{1}{1 + \frac{t^M}{x^M}\frac{\partial x^M}{\partial q^M} + \frac{t}{x^M}\frac{\partial x^d}{\partial q^M} + \frac{t_w \cdot w}{x^M}\frac{\partial L^s}{\partial q^M}} w dL^z \tag{5.38}$$

Thus, in this simple model, the tariff is evaluated in the same way as other distortionary taxes. This is most easily seen by setting $t = t_w = 0$, then (5.38) parallels (4.1). If the imported good is normal, then the MCPF exceeds one when there are no other distortionary taxes. Introducing a good that is exclusively exported and allowing the exchange rate to clear the current account would add $\left(x^E - x^M\right) de^R = 0$, where x^E denotes exports facing a world market price equal to one, e^R denotes the exchange rate, and the change in export income comes from the income argument of the indirect utility function (with $d\pi^E = x^E de^R + e^R dx^E - w dL^E = x^E de^R$).

The European Union will introduce a carbon border adjustment mechanism, CBAM. Those importing carbon-intensive products have to buy carbon certificates corresponding to the carbon price that would have been paid, had the goods been produced under the EU's carbon pricing rules. Conversely, once a non-EU producer can show that they have already paid a price for the carbon used in producing imported goods in a third country, the corresponding cost can be fully deducted for the EU importer.[18] Replacing the tax on emissions in Subsection 5.3 with an import tariff provides a simple way of evaluating the CBAM, if some of the revenue is used to finance projects within the union.

---

[18] https://ec.europa.eu/commission/presscorner/detail/en/qanda_21_3661. The Council of the EU adopted key pieces of legislation on April 25, 2023.

If the project under evaluation uses an imported good covered by the CBAM as an input, the tariff could be added to the project's upfront costs and multiplied by the MCPF in (5.10). This assumes that the tariff reflects the global damage cost. Alternatively, evaluate the cost in the way suggested below equation (5.10) in Subsection 5.3.

5.10 A Partial Equilibrium Approach

Thus far, all prices have been assumed to remain constant. In this subsection, this assumption is abandoned, and the goods price is endogenous. In the following subsection, we allow all relative prices to be flexible.

The indirect utility function is as follows:

$$V = V(z, q, w_d, m),\tag{5.39}$$

where $w_d = w$, and $m = \pi$, i.e., aggregate profit income, and $T = 0$. Consider now a small increase in the provision of z financed by raising the unit tax t:

$$\frac{dV}{V_m} = \frac{V_z}{V_m}dz - x^d \cdot (dp + dt) + x^s dp = \frac{V_z}{V_m}dz - x^d dt,\tag{5.40}$$

where $\partial \pi^x / \partial p = x^s$, the goods market clears, explaining that the expression can be simplified as on the right-hand side.

The government's only tax source is the unit tax. Hence, the considered project causes the following adjustment to the government's budget:

$$x^d dt + t\frac{\partial x^d}{\partial q}(dp + dt) + t\frac{\partial x^d}{\partial m}d\pi = wdL^z,\tag{5.41}$$

where $d\pi = x^s dp + pdx^s - wdL^d + 1 \cdot dx^{nu} - wdL^{nu} = x^s dp$ if firms are price-taking profit maximizers. Drawing on the Slutsky equation, the income effect in (5.41) can be eliminated. After some calculations, one obtains:

$$xdt = \left(wdL^z - t\frac{\partial x^{dH}}{\partial q}dp\right)\frac{1}{1 + t\frac{\partial x^d}{\partial q}},\tag{5.42}$$

where a superscript H denotes a Hicksian substitution effect; the positive income effect on demand of the price decrease is equal to the negative income effect due to the loss in profit income. Hence, only the substitution effect remains in (5.42). Using (5.42) in (5.40), we obtain:

$$\frac{dV}{V_m} = \frac{V_z}{V_m}dz - \left(wdL^z - t\frac{\partial x^{dH}}{\partial q}dp\right)\frac{1}{1 + t\frac{\partial x^d}{\partial q}}.\tag{5.43}$$

If the demand curve is downward sloping while the supply curve is upward sloping, the equilibrium price will fall; see equation (5.46). Thus, the project's total cost falls short of the one in equation (4.1), ceteris paribus. This is due to a gain on the tax base as the producer price decreases, which causes demand for the taxed good to increase. If $dp = 0$, then (5.43) reduces to (4.1), i.e., the total project cost is higher than when the producer price falls. If lump-sum taxation is available, while $t > 0$ is fixed and $t_w = 0$, then equation (3.4) is augmented by the substitution term in the numerator of (5.43).

Turning to the market price, use the equilibrium condition:

$$x^d(q, w_d, m) = x^s(p, w),\qquad(5.44)$$

where weak separability between z and other goods is maintained. Differentiating the expression, one obtains:

$$\frac{\partial x^d}{\partial q}(dp + dt) + \frac{\partial x^d}{\partial m}d\pi = \frac{\partial x^s}{\partial p}dp,\qquad(5.45)$$

where $d\pi = x^s dp$, and we can once again draw on the Slutsky equation on the left-hand side of the equation when the market is in equilibrium. Multiplying through by $1/dt$, solving for the price change caused by the tax hike, and multiplying both the numerator and the denominator by q/x^d, one has:

$$\frac{dp}{dt} = \frac{\frac{q}{x^d}\frac{\partial x^d}{\partial q}}{\frac{q}{x^d}\left(\frac{\partial x^s}{\partial p} - \frac{\partial x^{dH}}{\partial q}\right)} = \frac{\varepsilon^d}{\frac{q}{p}\varepsilon^s - \varepsilon^{dH}},\qquad(5.46)$$

where ε denotes a price elasticity. The supply-side price elasticity ε^s is positive, while both the ordinary and the Hicksian demand-side elasticity are negative, in general. Hence, typically, the equilibrium price is reduced.

Subsection A.5 of the Appendix outlines the case where the wage is endogenous.

5.11 A General Equilibrium Approach

Let us add a (slightly involved) general equilibrium CBA where all relative prices are flexible; the analysis is general equilibrium given the simple model employed in this subsection, but more general models include many goods, many produced inputs, different labor skills, and various capital goods. For simplicity, $t \geq 0$ is fixed while $t_w = 0$. The model has the same structure as before, namely two private goods, one serving as the numéraire, labor, and a public good. Using the equilibrium conditions for two markets, one can solve the system of equations to obtain $p = p(z)$ and $w = w(z)$, suppressing any other parameters, as is further illustrated by solving a numerical model in equations (5.48)–(5.52). Differentiating the indirect utility function, one obtains:

$$\frac{dV}{V_m} = \frac{V_z}{V_m}dz + \left(x^s - x^d\right)\frac{\partial p}{\partial z}dz + (L^s - L - L^z)\frac{\partial w}{\partial z}dz$$

$$- \left(w\frac{\partial L^z}{\partial z}dz - t\frac{\partial x^d}{\partial q}\frac{\partial p}{\partial z}dz - t\frac{\partial x^d}{\partial w}\frac{\partial w}{\partial z}dz - t\frac{\partial x^d}{\partial m}\frac{\partial m}{\partial z}dz\right)$$

$$= \left[\frac{V_z}{V_m} - \left(w\frac{\partial L^z}{\partial z} - t\frac{\partial x^d}{\partial q}\frac{\partial p}{\partial z} - t\frac{\partial x^d}{\partial w}\frac{\partial w}{\partial z} - t\frac{\partial x^d}{\partial m}\frac{\partial m}{\partial z}\right)\right]dz, \qquad (5.47)$$

where L denotes aggregate private sector demand for labor, prices clear markets, $m = \pi - T$ with $p = p(z)$, $w = w(z)$, and the final income effect within parentheses in the final line accounts for the change in T, caused by the change in z, except $L^z \cdot (\partial w/\partial z)dz$ which vanishes when the labor market clears; compare equations (5.48) and (5.49). (The expression can be further simplified because some income effects appear with opposite signs, but this simplification is not undertaken.) Thus, according to the final line of (5.47), the impact of the change in z on tax bases is deducted from the project's upfront cost evaluated at constant prices.

Alternatively, the "conventional" definition can be used to obtain:

$$\frac{dV}{V_m} = \frac{V_z}{V_m}dz - dT + (L^s - L)\,dw$$

$$= \frac{V_z}{V_m}dz - \left(wdL^z + L^z dw - t\cdot\frac{\partial x^d}{\partial q}dp - t\cdot\frac{\partial x^d}{\partial w}dw - t\cdot\frac{\partial x^d}{\partial m}d\pi\right)\cdot MCPF^T$$

$$+ (L^s - L)\,dw, \qquad (5.47')$$

where $dw = (\partial w/\partial z)dz$, and so on, and Subsection A.6 in the Appendix shows that $MCPF^T = 1/(1 - t\partial x^d/\partial m)$, i.e., looks like the MCPF in equation (3.7) when $t_w = 0$ also in the latter expression. If $t_w > 0$, then the MCPF formally replicates the one in (3.7), although the two typically are evaluated at different "points" or prices. In a general equilibrium perspective (5.47') seems to be no simple evaluation rule because one has to estimate the difference between labor supply and private sector demand for labor multiplied by the change in the wage rate; alternatively, replace the final term within parentheses by $L^z dw$. The reason is that one cannot "factor out" $L^z dw$ from the cost expression unless $MCPF^T$ is equal to one.

A numerical illustration is added in what follows. The direct utility function is assumed to be a logarithmic Cobb-Douglas function in all arguments but the public good, which has a logarithmic Stone-Geary type of function (such that the agent "survives" even if $z = 0$). The indirect utility function is as follows:

$$V = \ln\left(\frac{m + w\cdot TE}{3\cdot q}\right) + \ln\left(\frac{m + w\cdot TE}{3\cdot 1}\right) + \ln\left(TE - \frac{2\cdot w\cdot TE - m}{3\cdot w}\right) + \ln(z+1).$$

$$(5.48)$$

Thus, there are two private goods, out of which the second one serves as numéraire, untaxed labor, and a public good. The arguments within parentheses, except for TE and the minus sign following it, constitute the demand and labor supply functions. Lump-sum income equals the sum of the profit incomes less a lump-sum tax:

$$m = \frac{p^2}{4 \cdot w} + \frac{1}{4 \cdot w} - T, \tag{5.49}$$

where the first two terms on the right-hand side are profit functions of the firms supplying x and x^{nu}, respectively. Thus, there is just one firm in each market for private goods. The government's budget constraint is as follows:

$$T = w \cdot z^2 - t \cdot \frac{m + w \cdot \text{TE}}{3 \cdot q}, \tag{5.50}$$

where the production function for the public good is $z = (L^z)^{1/2}$. Using equation (5.50) to eliminate T from equation (5.49), the latter equation can be solved to obtain:

$$m = \frac{3 \cdot q \cdot \left(1 + p^2\right) + 4 \cdot t \cdot \text{TE} \cdot w^2 - 12 \cdot q \cdot w^2 \cdot z^2}{4 \cdot (3 \cdot q - t) \cdot w}. \tag{5.51}$$

Differentiating the profit functions with respect to p and w and using the demand and supply functions in the indirect utility function, one arrives at the following market equilibria:

$$\frac{p}{2 \cdot w} - \frac{m + w \cdot \text{TE}}{3 \cdot q} = 0$$

$$\frac{2 \cdot w \cdot \text{TE} - m}{3 \cdot w} - \frac{p^2}{4 \cdot w^2} - \frac{1}{4 \cdot w^2} - z^2 = 0. \tag{5.52}$$

The first line contains the supply function less the demand function for x. The second line covers the labor market, with z^2 denoting the public sector's demand for labor. The remaining market is in equilibrium if (5.52) is satisfied. After replacing m with the right-hand side in equation (5.51), one can solve (5.52) to obtain the general equilibrium prices p and w as functions of z. (Alternatively, add an equation for m to equation (5.52) and solve for p, w, and m.) Suppose that $t = 0$ and the TE equals 24. Then one obtains $p = 1$ and $w = 1/(24 - z^2)^{1/2}$. Thus, the larger z is, i.e., the more labor the public sector demands, the higher the equilibrium wage, while p is unaffected by the magnitude of z. Note that only relative prices matter for the firms. For $z = 1$, w is around 0.209.

Figure 3 illustrates that there is an interior optimum for the provision of the public good. This occurs for $z \approx 1.827$ when $t = t_w = 0$. A CBA confirms this; the difference between marginal benefits and marginal costs is virtually

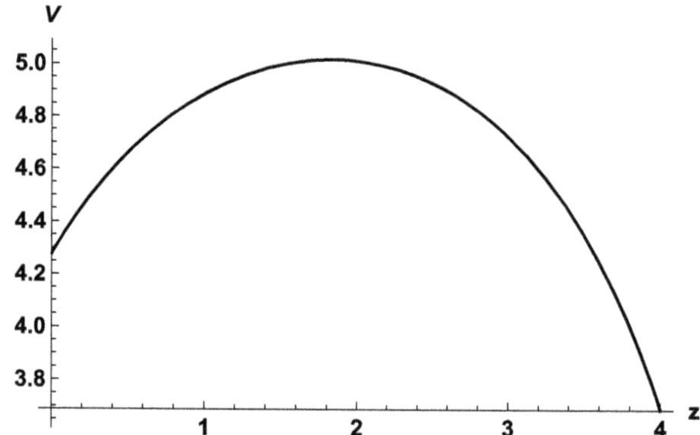

Figure 3 Welfare as a function of the provision of the public good

zero at $z = 1.827$ (with $V_m \approx 0.44$). Recall that MCPF $= 1$ because there is no distortionary taxation.

Suppose that t is increased from 0 to 0.1 while $z = 1$. Then, p is reduced to around 0.95 (while q increases to around 1.05). This reduces the private sector's demand for labor. Consequently, w drops to around 0.206 to restore equilibrium in the labor market. A general equilibrium evaluation around this "point" can be undertaken by calculating $(dV/dz)/V_m$. Take the partial derivative of equation (5.48) with respect to z using equation (5.49) and the price functions, and evaluate the resulting expression at $z = 1$, $t = 0.1$.[19] This outcome, based on unobservable utility items, should provide the correct answer and is stated in the first line in Table 1.

Next, undertake a CBA of marginally increasing z from one. The marginal utility benefit is obtained by taking the partial derivative of equation (5.48) with respect to z. It is converted to monetary units by division by the marginal utility of income. The (marginal) WTP is an expression that can be estimated using, for example, survey techniques. Use equation (5.51) in equation (5.50) and differentiate with respect to z using the price functions to obtain the cost change. However, to avoid double-counting $L^z \cdot (dw/dz)$ $(= 0.0089574)$ must be deducted and shifted to the equilibrium condition for the labor market, i.e., $\left(L^s - L^d - L^{nu} - L^z\right) dw/dz = 0$; compare equation (5.47).

Thus, the second line in Table 1, which contains the same terms as the final line in equation (5.47), reveals that the CBA produces the same surplus as when the evaluation is based on the utility function (but some decimals have been omitted in the middle equalities in the table). The total cost for the project is

---

[19] Given $t = 0.1$, p remains constant at around 0.951249, while $w = (1/20)\cdot((801 - 401^{(1/2)}/(48 - 2 \cdot z^2))^{(1/2)}$. Thus, w is an increasing function of z.

Table 1 Project appraisals

$(dV/dz)/V_m$	$= 0.326087/0.41204$	$= 0.791396$
CBA	$= 0.5/0.41204 - (0.431035 - 0.0089574)$	$= 0.791396$
CBA.1	$= 0.5/0.41204 + (0.41204 + 0.0089574$	$= 0.791396$
	$\quad - 0.00362987) \cdot 1.03275 + 0.0089574$	

equal to the direct one ($= 2 \cdot w \cdot 1 = 0.41204$) multiplied by 1.0243, i.e., there is still an MCPF.

Defining the MCPF as in equation (3.4) in Section 3, but with $t_w = 0$, yields $MCPF^T \approx 1.03275$. Based on equation (5.47'), the marginal cost in the final line of Table 1 equals $[2 \cdot w + L^z \partial w/\partial z - t \cdot (\partial x^d/\partial z)] \cdot MCPF^T$, where $\partial x^d/\partial z$ refers to changes in the demand for the commodity as prices and income adjust as z changes; recall that p, w, and m are functions of z. Computed in this way, the total marginal cost is around 0.431035, but there is an additional benefit due to the increase in the wage times L^z. If this benefit is accounted for, also this approach provides the correct answer. If the MCPF was equal to one, the two terms $L^z \hat{\partial} w/\hat{\partial} z (= 0.0089574)$ appear with opposite signs and hence sum to zero. In any case, equation (5.47) seems slightly easier to approximate than equation (5.47').[20]

Based on the EV concept, Johansson (2021) derives cost–benefit rules for large projects in closed and open economies. One approach "collapses" the economy-wide effects into a single market (but a term reflecting any market distortions must be added). It could be seen as a discrete and more general variation of (5.47). The other approach allocates gains and losses to various stakeholders sequentially (based on a line integral). The discrete tax wedge terms in Johansson's (2021) equations (A.1) and (A.2) could be rewritten to provide an MCPF expression for a large project, just as done for a small project in equation (5.47'). Refer also to Kotchen and Levison (2022), who examine the sign of welfare effects of large projects in secondary markets. In (5.47), the market for the taxed private good is a secondary market.

6 Extension to a World with Many Goods and Factors and to an Intertemporal World

In this section, the basic model is extended to a world with many goods and factors and to an intertemporal world. The first subsection provides a

---

[20] If lump-sum taxation is ruled out, the monetary surplus is somewhat reduced. In this case, $x^d \partial t/\partial z - L^z \partial w/\partial z$ is equal to the terms within parentheses in the final line of equation (5.47). Once again, also the "conventional" approach, where the MCPF is estimated as in equation (4.1), results in the correct answer.

generalization to the case where there are many commodities and types of labor. The second subsection provides a simple intertemporal extension of the Ramsey model. Finally, a more general case with many goods and factors in an intertemporal world is considered.

6.1 Extending the Basic Model to Many Goods and Factors

Let us begin by generalizing to the case where there are $n+1$ commodities and k types of labor. Select commodity 0 as an untaxed numéraire and normalize its price to one. A straightforward generalization of the simple model employed in Sections 3–5 is as follows. Let us make the following interpretations: $t = [t_1, \ldots, t_n]$ and $\partial x^d / \partial m = [\partial x_1^d / \partial m, \ldots, \partial x_n^d / \partial m]$. The transpose of $\partial x^d / \partial m$ is a column vector, i.e., having n rows and a single column ($n \times 1$), vector multiplication yields:

$$t \frac{\partial x^{dT}}{\partial m} = t_1 \frac{\partial x_1^d}{\partial m} + \cdots + t_n \frac{\partial x_n^d}{\partial m}, \tag{6.1}$$

where T refers to the transpose of $\partial x^d / \partial m$. Proceeding in a parallel way for labor, one obtains:

$$t_w \cdot w \frac{\partial L^{sT}}{\partial m} = t_{w1} \cdot w_1 \frac{\partial L_1^s}{\partial m} + \cdots + t_{wk} \cdot w_k \frac{\partial L_k^s}{\partial m}. \tag{6.2}$$

Thus, in terms of equation (3.4), we simply replace $t \partial x^d / \partial m$ and $t_w \cdot w \partial L^s / \partial m$ by the right-hand sides of equations (6.1) and (6.2), respectively.

The tax vector could be such that there is a VAT. Then, interpret taxes as ad valorem, multiply t_i by p_i, and set $t_i = t^{VAT}$ for $i = 1, \ldots, n$. (If all $n+1$ consumer goods are subject to the tax and there is a single type of labor, taxing consumer goods (but not labor) is equivalent to taxing labor income at the rate $(1+t^{VAT})^{-1}$). Alternatively, some tax rates might be strictly positive, some equal to zero, and some strictly negative, i.e., some commodities might be subsidized. Similarly, taxes could vary across different types of labor, and some types might even be subsidized.

One could make a similar interpretation of the Ramsey case. However, it is worthwhile to elaborate somewhat on this case. The indirect utility function is stated as:

$$V\left(z, p_1 + t_1, \ldots, p_n + t_n, w_1 \cdot (1 - t_{w_1}), \ldots, w_k \cdot (1 - t_{w_k}), m^{To}\right), \tag{6.3}$$

where $m^{To} = \pi^{To}$ is interpreted as the total profit income generated by the $n+1$ sectors. The government's budget constraint is stated as follows:

$$\Sigma_{i=1}^n t_i \cdot \left(x_i^d + x_i^z\right) + \Sigma_{i=1}^k t_{w_i} \cdot w_i \cdot L_i^s - \Sigma_{i=1}^n (p_i + t_i) \cdot x_i^z - \Sigma_{i=1}^k w_i \cdot L_i^z = 0. \tag{6.4}$$

Note that the taxes paid by the project constitute revenue to the government and hence sum to zero. For notational simplicity, it is ignored that producing the public good might also require the numéraire as an input.

Suppose the unit tax on commodity j is used to finance the small project under scrutiny. In the absence of lump-sum taxation, and if all producer prices p_i and w_i remain constant, then the change in monetary welfare equals:

$$\frac{dV}{V_m} = \frac{V_z}{V_m} dz - x_j dt_j. \tag{6.5}$$

The change in the government's budget equals:

$$x_j^d dt_j + \Sigma_{i=1}^n t_i \frac{\partial x_i^d}{\partial q_j} dt_j + \Sigma_{i=1}^k t_{w_i} \cdot w_i \frac{\partial L_i^s}{\partial q_j} dt_j - \Sigma_{i=1}^n p_i dx_i^z - \Sigma_{i=1}^k w_i dL_i^z = 0. \tag{6.6}$$

This equation can be stated as follows:

$$\left[1 + \Sigma_{i=1}^n \frac{t_i}{x_j} \frac{\partial x_i^d}{\partial q_j} + \Sigma_{i=1}^k \frac{t_{w_i} \cdot w_i}{x_j} \frac{\partial L_i^s}{\partial q_j}\right] \cdot x_j^d dt_j = \Sigma_{i=1}^n p_i dx_i^z + \Sigma_{i=1}^k w_i dL_i^z. \tag{6.6'}$$

Thus, we arrive at the following cost–benefit rule:

$$\frac{dV}{V_m} = \frac{V_z}{V_m} dz - \left[\Sigma_{i=1}^n p_i dx_i^z + \Sigma_{i=1}^k w_i dL_i^z\right] \cdot \frac{1}{1 + \Sigma_{i=1}^n \frac{t_i}{x_j} \frac{\partial x_i^d}{\partial q_j} + \Sigma_{i=1}^k \frac{t_{w_i} \cdot w_i}{x_j} \frac{\partial L_i^s}{\partial q_j}}. \tag{6.7}$$

Without lump-sum taxes, this rule provides a straightforward generalization of equation (4.1) in Section 4. If a tax on w_j is used to finance the project, one would replace x_j with L_j^s in (6.7) and take the derivatives with respect to w_{dj} (instead of q_j), which reverses the signs of all tax elasticities. If only labor is taxed, one arrives at a straightforward generalization of equation (4.2) in Section 4.

It is hard to distill any simple rules for optimal taxation unless quite restrictive assumptions are introduced. A VAT is typically not optimal, i.e., differentiated taxation is preferred, in general. In any case, a change in the VAT is a bit complicated to evaluate because each demand and supply is affected by n consumer price changes. However, a possible simplification is as follows. Interpret x^d as an aggregate (nondurable) composite consumption commodity, i.e., a proxy for real (nondurable) private consumption, and t as the average tax rate on such private consumption. If one can find price and income/expenditure elasticities for real private consumption (or aggregate across commodity groups), a simple estimate of the MCPF is obtained.

For good reviews of optimal taxation, the reader is referred to Auerbach and Hines (2002, pp. 1361–71), Hindriks and Myles (2005, Ch. 15), and Myles (1995, pp. 190–192).

6.2 A Simple Intertemporal Extension of the Basic Model

In this subsection, the Ramsey-type model with a unit tax on one commodity is extended from a single period to multiple periods, but all decisions are taken at the beginning of the first period. Thus, the agent maximizes a utility function subject to the intertemporal present value budget constraint. Alternatively, the dynamic programming method breaks down the problem into a sequence of two-period optimization problems. The choice variables are chosen sequentially (recursively) rather than simultaneously. For the kind of problems considered in this section of the Element, it is sufficient to stick to the "Lagrangian" approach (and dynamic programming requires a time-additive and separable objective function). Refer to Stokey and Lucas (1989) for the seminal work on dynamic programming methods.

The agent has a labor income that, in period 1, is split between consumption and savings, denoted $s_1 > 0$. Interest is received at the beginning of period 2, and wage income plus $s_1 \cdot (1+r)$, where r denotes the interest rate, is consumed in the second, final period, i.e., $s_2 = 0$. Thus, initially, a two-period case is considered. If, instead, the agent borrows in period 1, then the loan plus interest is repaid in period 2. Multiplying through the period 2 budget constraint by $(1+r)^{-1}$ converts second-period prices and wages to present values at the beginning of period 1. Suppressing any lump-sum income, the intertemporal present value budget constraint is as follows:

$$w_{d1} \cdot L_1 + w_{d2} \cdot L_2 - q_{11} \cdot x_{11} - 1 \cdot x_{10}^{nu} - q_{21} \cdot x_{21} - \frac{1}{1+r} \cdot x_{20}^{nu} = 0, \quad (6.8)$$

where $x_{\tau 0}^{nu}$ denotes the numéraire good, whose end-user price here is set equal to one in both periods, $q_{\tau 1} = (p_{\tau 1} + t_{\tau 1})$ and $W_{d\tau} = w_\tau \cdot (1 - t_{w\tau})$ denote present values at the beginning of the first period for $\tau = 1, 2$. In what follows $t_{w\tau} = 0$ for all τ. Maximizing the direct utility function:

$$U = U\left(z_1, z_2, x_{10}^{nu}, x_{20}^{nu}, x_{11}, x_{21}, \text{TE} - L_1, \text{TE} - L_2\right), \quad (6.9)$$

subject to the budget constraint (6.8) yields the indirect utility function:

$$V(z_1, z_2, q_{11}, q_{21}, w_{d1}, w_{d2}), \quad (6.10)$$

where the numéraire prices are suppressed. The government's budget constraint equals:

$$\sum_{\tau=1}^{2} \left[t_\tau \cdot x_{\tau 1}^d - w_\tau \cdot L_\tau^z\right] = 0. \quad (6.11)$$

Suppose that the commodity taxes are used to finance the considered project, while as mentioned above equation (6.9), labor taxes are set equal to zero. Then, the change in monetary welfare caused by a marginal change in the provision of the public good equals:

$$\frac{dV}{V_m} = \frac{V_{z_1}}{V_m}dz_1 + \frac{V_{z_2}}{V_m}dz_2 - x_{11}^d dt_{11} - x_{21}^d dt_{21}, \tag{6.12}$$

where V_m is obtained by adding a present value lump-sum income to equations (6.8) and (6.10). Next, differentiate the government's budget constraint. After some calculations, one obtains:

$$x_{11}^d dt_{11}\left[1 + \frac{t_{11}}{x_{11}^d}\frac{\partial x_{11}^d}{\partial q_{11}} + \frac{t_{21}}{x_{11}^d}\frac{\partial x_{21}^d}{\partial q_{11}}\right]$$

$$+ x_{21}^d dt_{21}\left[1 + \frac{t_{21}}{x_{21}^d}\frac{\partial x_{21}^d}{\partial q_{21}} + \frac{t_{11}}{x_{21}^d}\frac{\partial x_{11}^d}{\partial q_{21}}\right] - w_1 dL_1^z - w_2 dL_2^z = 0. \tag{6.13}$$

If the present value taxes are chosen optimally, subject to being strictly positive, the two expressions within square brackets will have equal magnitude. To see this, according to equation (6.12), monetary welfare remains unchanged by a marginal tax reform if $x_{11}^d dt_{11} = -x_{21}^d dt_{21}$. Next, from equation (6.13), tax revenue will be unchanged if the two expressions within brackets are of equal size; recall that in terms of a Laffer curve, reducing a high tax means a small loss of tax revenue while raising a low tax produces a large increase in tax revenue. Then, multiplying through (6.13) by one over the first expression within square brackets and using the resulting expression in equation (6.12), the cost–benefit rule reads:

$$\frac{dV}{V_m} = \sum_\tau \left(\frac{V_{z_\tau}}{V_m}dz_\tau\right) - \left(\sum_\tau w_\tau dL_\tau^Z\right)\frac{1}{1 + \frac{t_{11}}{x_{11}^d}\frac{\partial x_{11}^d}{\partial q_{11}} + \frac{t_{21}}{x_{11}^d}\frac{\partial x_{21}^d}{\partial q_{11}}}, \tag{6.14}$$

where $\tau, j = 1, 2, \tau \neq j$, and one could as well multiply through by one over the second expression within square brackets in (6.13). Thus, the sum of the direct present-value marginal costs over time is multiplied by the common present value MCPF and summed. The second-period marginal value of the public good is discounted through the "form" of the indirect utility function. For example, if the utility function is time-separable, the second-period function might be something like $\delta \cdot v(.)$, where $\delta = (1 + \gamma)^{-1}$ and γ denotes the utility discount rate. Thus, $V_{z_2} = \delta \cdot v_{z_2}$. In any case, the approach employed in this subsection provides a straightforward generalization of the single-period case. The corresponding optimization problem is outlined in Subsection A.7 of the Appendix, and the condition that must be satisfied in each period if the aim is to maximize social welfare in a second-best world is stated. If the number of periods is extended, one simply extends the time horizon in equation (6.14) from two periods to the desired number of periods.

The implication for empirical CBA seems to be that the present value of the MCPF must be the same over time, and the tax used to finance the project must be optimal in each period. Otherwise, it seems almost impossible to arrive at a cost–benefit rule that can be estimated.

However, a catcher in the rye is provided by a tax change that is uniform over time. Then, one obtains:

$$MCPF^t = 1/\left[1 + \frac{t}{x_{11}^d + x_{21}^d}\frac{\partial x_{11}^d}{\partial q_{11}} + \frac{t}{x_{11}^d + x_{21}^d}\frac{\partial x_{21}^d}{\partial q_{11}} + \frac{t}{x_{11}^d + x_{21}^d}\frac{\partial x_{21}^d}{\partial q_{21}} \right. $$
$$\left. + \frac{t}{x_{11}^d + x_{21}^d}\frac{\partial x_{11}^d}{\partial q_{21}}\right], \tag{6.15}$$

where $dt_{11} = dt_{21}$ denotes equal-sized present value tax adjustments in (6.13). Thus, this approach provides a weighted average of the expressions within square brackets in equation (6.13). This rule, too, can be extended to cover an average over an arbitrary number of periods.

An even simpler outcome occurs if just one tax is adjusted to finance the project. Then, either dt_{11} or dt_{21} equals zero in equation (6.13).

A remaining issue relates to time or dynamic inconsistency (Strotz, 1955). Consider the optimal consumption of a good across two periods. If the optimal consumption in period 2 matches the level forecasted in period 1, then the time 1 plan is time-consistent. Otherwise, it is time-inconsistent. If the present value MCPF is time-dependent, it might turn out that a project that is socially unprofitable if launched today is socially profitable if undertaken at some future point in time or vice versa. For example, if the real MCPF declines (sufficiently fast) over time the outcome seems to remind of the one occurring under hyperbolic discounting, i.e., results in a kind of time inconsistency; see, for example, Harstad (2020). However, while dynamic inconsistency is due to changing preferences over time, "fund inconsistency" is due to raising funds by nonoptimal taxation.[21]

It might be mentioned that some authors prefer to use different social discount rates for environmental commodities and other commodities. The idea is that future generations will experience a poorer environmental quality. Hence, environmental commodities should be discounted at a lower rate than other consumption. Refer to Nesticò et al. (2023) for further discussion of such dual discounting.

---

[21] Given exponential discounting, the marginal rate of substitution of consumption (MRS) between two consecutive periods equals $1/(1 + r)$. In the case of hyperbolic discounting, say, $1/(1 + c \cdot \tau)$, where $c > 0$, the MRS will tend to unity for two consecutive periods far in the future.

6.3 A More General Intertemporal Model

In this subsection, the model introduced in Subsection 5.1 is generalized to an arbitrary number of commodities, labor categories, and periods. Suppose that there are N periods. Then, the indirect utility function of the representative agent can be stated as follows:

$$V = V\left(z, p_{11} + t_1, \ldots, p_{Nn} + t_{Nn}, w_{11} \cdot \left(1 - t_{w_{11}}\right), \ldots, w_{Nk} \cdot \left(1 - t_{w_{Nk}}\right), \pi^{PV}\right)$$

$$= V\left(z, q_{11}, \ldots, q_{Nn}, w_{d11}, \ldots, w_{dNk}, m^{PV}\right), \tag{6.16}$$

where $z = [z_1, \ldots, z_N]$ denotes a vector of provisions of the public good in each of the N periods, the assumption that preferences are weakly separable in the public good and other goods is maintained, all monetary entities are expressed as present values at the beginning of the first period, and $m^{PV} = \pi^{PV}$, where π^{PV} denotes total present value profits, and lump-sum taxation is ruled out.

The government's budget constraint is as follows:

$$\sum_{\tau=1}^{N} \sum_{i=1}^{n} t_{\tau i} \cdot \left(x_{\tau i}^d + x_{\tau i}^z\right) + \sum_{\tau=1}^{N} \sum_{i=1}^{k} t_{w_{\tau i}} \cdot L_{\tau i}^S$$

$$- \sum_{\tau=1}^{N} \sum_{i=1}^{n^z} (p_{\tau i} + t_{\tau i}) \cdot x_{\tau i}^z - \sum_{\tau=1}^{N} \sum_{i=1}^{k^z} w_{\tau i} \cdot L_{\tau i}^z = 0, \tag{6.17}$$

where $n^z \subseteq n$ and $k^z \subseteq k$ because the project will most likely demand only strict subsets of the available inputs. As before, taxes paid by the producer of the public good are revenue to the Ministry of Finance; hence, sum to zero.

Suppose that the provision of the public good is marginally increased in each of the N periods. The tax on, say, the first commodity is adjusted in each period to cover the cost of the increased provision of z, while, for notational simplicity, labor is untaxed; one of the commodity taxes must be endogenous and balance the government's budget. Monetary welfare is changed in the following way:

$$\frac{dV}{V_m} = \sum_{\tau=1}^{N} \frac{V_{z_\tau}}{V_m} dz_\tau - \sum_{\tau=1}^{N} x_{\tau 1}^d dt_{\tau 1}. \tag{6.18}$$

Next, consider the (ceteris paribus) impact on tax revenue of dt_{11}. One obtains:

$$x_{11}^d dt_{11} + \sum_{\tau=1}^{N} \sum_{i=1}^{n} t_{\tau i} \frac{\partial x_{\tau i}^d}{\partial q_{11}} dt_{11} = x_{11}^d dt_{11} \left(1 + \sum_{\tau=1}^{N} \sum_{i=1}^{n} \frac{t_{\tau i}}{x_{11}^d} \frac{\partial x_{\tau i}^d}{\partial q_{11}}\right).$$

$$\tag{6.19}$$

Thus, demand for each out of n commodities in each out of N periods is affected (although not all derivatives need to differ from zero). Next, assume that the tax on the first commodity is raised in all N periods. Then, adding the considered public sector project, one obtains:

$$x_{11}^d dt_{11} \left[1 + \sum_{\tau=1}^{N} \sum_{i=1}^{n} \frac{t_{\tau i}}{x_{11}^d} \frac{\partial x_{\tau i}^d}{\partial q_{11}} \right] + \cdots + x_{N1}^d dt_{N1}$$

$$\times \left[1 + \sum_{\tau=1}^{N} \sum_{i=1}^{n} \frac{t_{\tau i}}{x_{N1}^d} \frac{\partial x_{\tau i}^d}{\partial q_{N1}} \right] = \sum_{\tau=1}^{N} \sum_{i=1}^{n^z} p_{\tau i} dx_{\tau i}^z$$

$$+ \sum_{\tau=1}^{N} \sum_{i=1}^{k^z} w_{\tau i} dL_{\tau i}^z. \tag{6.20}$$

Thus, if all N expressions within square brackets are equal, one can multiply through by one over an arbitrarily chosen expression. Then, the tax change terms in equation (6.18) can be replaced by the project cost divided by the chosen expression to obtain:

$$\frac{dV}{V_m} = \sum_{\tau=1}^{N} \frac{V_{z_\tau}}{V_m} dz_\tau - \left(\sum_{\tau=1}^{N} \sum_{i=1}^{n^z} p_{\tau i} dx_{\tau i}^z + \sum_{\tau=1}^{N} \sum_{i=1}^{k^z} w_{\tau i} dL_{\tau i}^z \right)$$

$$\times \frac{1}{1 + \sum_{\tau=1}^{N} \sum_{i=1}^{n} \frac{t_{\tau i}}{x_{j1}^d} \frac{\partial x_{\tau i}^d}{\partial q_{j1}}} \tag{6.18'}$$

where $j \in [1, \ldots, N]$. Thus, at a second-best optimum, the present value MCPF must remain constant over time. Social welfare is maximized by scaling the provision of the public good such that the marginal WTP equals marginal cost, including the MCPF, in each period. The Samuelson rule is replicated if all distortionary taxes are equal to zero (and lump-sum taxation is reintroduced).

For extensions of the MCPF to growing economies, refer to Dahlby (2008) and Hashimzade and Myles (2014).

7 Optimal and Nonoptimal Income Distributions

In a multi-agent economy, typically, it is assumed that the government maximizes a social welfare function $W = W(V^1, \ldots, V^H)$. If the government can design individual lump-sum taxes (and set $t = t_w = 0$), it is possible to redistribute incomes such that:

$$\frac{\partial W}{\partial V^h} \frac{\partial V^h}{\partial m^h} = W_V^h \cdot V_m^h = \lambda \qquad \forall h, \tag{7.1}$$

where $\partial W / \partial V^h = W_V^h$ denotes the marginal welfare weight attributed to agent h for $h = 1, \ldots, H$, V_m^h denotes the marginal utility of income of agent h, and λ denotes a Lagrange multiplier connected to the government's budget constraint. For example, in a Utilitarian society, the marginal welfare weight equals unity for all agents, while in an inequality-adverse society, W_V^h is a decreasing function of utility (and in a Rawlsian society there is a corner solution in the sense that all agents, but the poorest one, are attributed a zero weight). Provided an interior solution exists, in this "ideal" case all agents are attributed the same welfare-adjusted marginal utility of income, i.e., λ, and we can proceed as if there is a single, representative agent. Then, the MCPF equals one (because the distortionary taxes must equal zero when (7.1) holds). Equivalently, one could interpret λ as equal to V_m in the previous sections of this Element, where $W_V^h = 1$.

7.1 A Simple Distributional Analysis

In this subsection, a simple distributional analysis is undertaken. However, let us begin by stating the Lagrangian to the considered maximization problem. This is done to define the MCPF in an economy with many agents. Suppose there are H agents and that the social welfare function is Utilitarian. The Lagrangian is stated as follows:

$$F(.) = \sum_h V^h\left(z, q, w_d, \pi^h - T\right)$$
$$+ \lambda \cdot \left(H \cdot T + \sum_h \left(t \cdot x^{hd} + t_w \cdot w \cdot L^{hs}\right) - w \cdot L^z\right). \tag{7.2}$$

Here, we assume only *uniform* lump-sum taxation is possible on the margin. This rules out the first-best solution indicated in equation (7.1). Assuming that preferences are weakly separable in the public good and other goods, first-order conditions for an interior solution, when $t > 0$ and $t_w = 0$, are:

$$\frac{\partial F}{\partial T} = -\sum_h V_m^h + \lambda \cdot \left(H - t \cdot \sum_h \frac{\partial x^{hd}}{\partial m_h}\right) = 0$$

$$\frac{\partial F}{\partial z} = \sum_h V_z^h - \lambda \cdot w \cdot \frac{\partial L^z}{\partial z} = 0$$

$$\frac{\partial F}{\partial \lambda} = H \cdot T + \sum_h t \cdot x^{hd} - w \cdot L^z = 0. \tag{7.3}$$

If $t = 0$ in (7.3), then the first line reduces to:

$$\lambda = \sum_h \frac{V_m^h}{H} = \bar{V}_m, \tag{7.4}$$

where $\bar{V}_m = E[V_m^h]$ denotes the average or expected private marginal utility of income. Multiply $\partial F/\partial z$ in (7.3) by $1/\bar{V}_m$ to convert the expression to monetary units. It follows that the MCPF, i.e., $\lambda/\bar{V}_m$ equals one.

If $t > 0$ in (7.3), then the first line reveals that:

$$\frac{\lambda}{\bar{V}_m} = \frac{1}{1 - t \cdot \frac{1}{H} \cdot \sum_h \frac{\partial x^{hd}}{\partial m^h}}. \tag{7.5}$$

This provides a straightforward generalization of equation (3.7) when $t_w = 0$. If the proportional income tax is positive, then the average labor supply income effect times $t_w \cdot w$ is deducted from the denominator of (7.5). By the way, $\lambda/\overline{V}_m$ is the definition of the MCPF suggested by Sandmo (1998).

Next, let us add a simple distributional analysis. Denote the marginal WTP of agent h for the public good $b^h = V_z^h/V_m^h$. Then, the optimal provision of the public good can be stated as:

$$\frac{\Sigma_h V_m^h b^h}{\overline{V}_m} dz = H\frac{E\left[V_m^h b^h\right]}{\overline{V}_m} dz = H\left[1 + \frac{\mathrm{cov}\left(V_m^h, b^h\right)}{\overline{V}_m E\left[b^h\right]}\right] E\left[b^h\right] dz$$

$$= \frac{\lambda}{\overline{V}_m}\left[wdL^z - \sum_h t\frac{\partial x^{hd}}{\partial z}dz\right], \tag{7.6}$$

where, for notational simplicity, $t_w = 0$, and $\mathrm{cov}(.) = E\left[V_m^h b^h\right] - \overline{V}_m E\left[b^h\right]$, which explains that the final product of the means must be added to the covariance term in the middle equality of the equation (and equals one after division by the denominator in the expression).[22] The ratio farthest to the left yields the sum of marginal WTPs for the public good using the average marginal utility of income to convert the expression from utility units to monetary units. The second ratio provides a kind of average, where the numerator equals the first part of the covariance, hence it must be multiplied by H, the number of agents. The covariance in the third equality is used to capture the distributional characteristic of the public good. Welfare weighting leads to a lower measure of benefits than simply summing WTPs if the covariance between the marginal utility of income and the marginal WTP is negative (Sandmo, 1998). If individualized lump-sum taxes are feasible, see equation (7.1), the marginal utility of income is evened out across agents (with $t = t_w = 0$). Hence, at the optimum, the sum of marginal WTPs equals the direct project cost because $MCPF = \lambda/V_m = 1$, where V_m denotes the common marginal utility of income.

The sum within the final square brackets in (7.6) can be moved to the benefit side because it is a function of z. In the single-agent case, Gahvari (2006, p. 1254) refers to the resulting expression as the marginal benefit of public goods, MBPG; also refer to Slemrod and Yitzhaki (2001). Then, at a second-best optimum MBPG = MCPF. This Element, which focuses on the cost side, assumes that the utility function is (weakly) separable in the public good and other goods. Hence, the covariance equals zero – V_m^h and b^h become uncorrelated – and the same holds for the sum within square brackets on the right-hand side of equation (7.6). In any case, as revealed by equation (7.6), the project's costs are multiplied by the MCPF. Distributional considerations, if any, can be shifted to the benefit side.

---

[22] With $t = 0$ and $t_w > 0$, the final term within brackets on the right-hand side of equation (7.2) is replaced by the sum across agents of $-t_w \cdot w \cdot \left(\partial L^{hs}/\partial z\right) dz$.

However, this last claim assumes that uniform lump-sum taxation is available. Suppose instead that the unit tax on consumption of x is used to finance a small expansion of the provision of the public good (and that preferences are weakly separable in z and other goods). After some calculations, one arrives at the following evaluation rule:

$$\sum_h \frac{dV^h}{\bar{V}_m} = \sum_h \frac{V_z^h}{\bar{V}_m} dz - wdL^z \frac{1}{1 + \frac{t}{\bar{x}^d}\frac{\partial \bar{x}^d}{\partial q}} - H \cdot \frac{\mathrm{cov}\left(V_m^h, x^{hd}\right)}{\bar{V}_m} dt, \qquad (7.6')$$

where a bar denotes an expected value, and the benefit side is kept as simple as possible because the focus here is on the cost side. To arrive at the cost side of (7.6'), differentiate $V^h(.)$ with respect to t to obtain $-V_m^h \cdot x^{hd} dt$, and use the fact that the sum across H agents equals $-H \cdot E\left[V_m^h \cdot x^{hd}\right] dt$. In turn, the latter equals $-H \cdot E\left[V_m^h\right] \cdot E\left[x^{hd}\right] dt = -H \cdot \bar{V}_m \cdot \bar{x}^d dt$ minus their covariance, as defined in (7.6'), multiplied by Hdt. Next, the government's budget constraint is used to obtain an expression for $-H \cdot \bar{x}^d dt$ that equals the upfront project cost times the MCPF, as defined in equation (7.6'). Now, the average tax elasticity appears in the MCPF, but the structure is the same as in the single-agent case considered in equation (4.1). However, (7.6') also involves a covariance term, which could be interpreted as a kind of distributional characteristic; dividing by the average marginal utility of income converts the expression to monetary units. If the marginal utility of income decreases as demand (a possible proxy for income) increases, the covariance term is negative. It equals zero if there is no link/correlation between the variables. Thus, it does not seem unlikely that the covariance term has a nonnegative impact on the project's social profitability. If so, ceteris paribus, an evaluation ignoring the covariance term, seems to provide a lower bound for social profitability.

If the income tax is increased (with $t = T = 0$), then minus the average labor tax elasticity appears in the denominator of the MCPF, and L^{hs} appears in the covariance term which now is multiplied by $H \cdot wdt_w$.

A slight generalization of the results follows if the weighted sum of private marginal utilities of income is replaced by the weighted sum of the social marginal welfare utility of income of each income group, i.e., $W_V^h \cdot V_m^h$. Needless to say, these averages are difficult to estimate. A possibility is to assume that:

$$W = \sum_h \frac{\left(\alpha^h \cdot V^h\right)^{1-\phi}}{1 - \phi} \qquad (7.1')$$

If the parameter $\phi = 0$ and the weights $\alpha^h = 1$ for all h, equation (7.1') reduces to the simple Utilitarian welfare function. As $\phi \to 1$ with $\alpha^h = 1$ for all h, the function reduces to the Bernoulli-Nash (Cobb-Douglas) function, while as $\phi \to \infty$, the limiting case is the Rawlsian social welfare function, where only the poorest group is attributed a positive weight. Refer to, for example, Boadway and Bruce (1984) for further details. A function like the one in (7.1') could be used in an empirical evaluation to illustrate how distributional assumptions affect the outcome.

Johansson and Kriström (2016, pp. 131–34) discuss how a few leading hands-on manuals handle the distributional issue. The European Commission's DG Regional Policy Unit's cost–benefit manual (European Commission, 2014), the UK's Green Book (HM Treasury, 2011), and the US Environmental Protection Agency's manual (US EPA 2010) are considered. Loomis (2011) provides a good overview of different ways of incorporating distributional issues in empirical CBA, and also discusses two empirical studies that handle distributional issues in different ways. Distributional comparative statics is the study of how individual decisions and equilibrium outcomes vary with changes in the distribution of economic parameters (income, wealth, productivity, information, and so on). Jensen (2018) develops new tools to address such issues and illustrates their usefulness in applications. Fleurbaey and Hammitt (2024) discuss various ways of accounting for distributional issues. They argue that an approach linking the CBA to a social welfare function is to be preferred. According to Brent (2023), many CBA practitioners have ignored using distribution weights, therefore inadequate attention has been given to how they can be estimated. One objective of Brent (2023) is to highlight the main methods for estimating these weights and to present applications of these methods.

7.2 A Sketch of a Simple Mirrlees Model

Another line of development draws on the optimal tax approach launched by Mirrlees (1971). Households are heterogeneous with respect to earning ability. However, the taxman cannot observe ability and working hours but has information on before-tax incomes. There are resource constraints and constraints relating to self-selection or incentive compatibility. The latter constraints are imposed to ensure that it is beneficial for an agent to choose the bundle of goods intended for her rather than choosing another bundle. According to the complex Mirrlees model, the marginal tax rate should be zero at the top if the skill distribution is bounded. If the marginal tax rate is zero at the top, it suggests that a marginal project could be financed in such a way that MCPF equals one. (Stern (1982) demonstrates that in a model with endogenous wages, the optimal income tax on the more skilled is negative and the tax on the less skilled is positive, in contrast to the standard results with exogenous wages.)

In closing this section, a sketch and discussion of the MCPF in a simple Mirrlees type of model is provided, drawing on Gahvari (2006). Suppose there are just two equal-sized groups of agents whose utility functions are separable in labor and other goods. Both consume a single private good, a public good, and supply labor. The total number of agents is normalized to unity. The two groups of agents differ in earning capacities, but there is asymmetric information, implying that the taxman can only observe pre-tax incomes. The after-tax income should not be such that an agent benefits from appearing as the other type of agent. Hence, there are self-selection constraints:

$$U^1\left(x^1,z\right) + u^1\left(\frac{I^1}{w}\right) \geq U^1\left(x^2,z\right) + u^1\left(\frac{I^2}{w}\right)$$

$$U^2\left(x^2,z\right) + u^2\left(\frac{I^2}{w}\right) \geq U^2\left(x^1,z\right) + u^2\left(\frac{I^1}{w}\right), \tag{7.7}$$

where $I^h = w \cdot L^s$, superscripts refer to types, and w is suppressed in what follows. The objective is to maximize a well-behaved Utilitarian social welfare function, subject to a resource constraint and the two self-selection constraints. The associated Lagrangian is as follows:

$$F(.) = 0.5 \cdot \left[U^1\left(x^1,z\right) + u^1\left(I^1\right)\right] + 0.5 \cdot \left[U^2\left(x^2,z\right) + u^2\left(I^2\right)\right]$$

$$+ \lambda \cdot 0.5 \cdot \left[I^1 - x^1 + I^2 - x^2 - \frac{w \cdot L^z}{0.5}\right]$$

$$+ \mu^{12} \cdot \left[U^1\left(x^1,z\right) + u^1\left(I^1\right) - U^1\left(x^2,z\right) - u^1\left(I^2\right)\right]$$

$$+ \mu^{21} \cdot \left[U^2\left(x^2,z\right) + u^2\left(I^2\right) - U^2\left(x^1,z\right) - u^2\left(I^1\right)\right], \tag{7.8}$$

where λ, μ^{12}, and μ^{21} denote Lagrange multipliers. Some first-order conditions for an interior solution are as follows:

$$\frac{\partial F}{\partial x^h} = 0.5 \cdot U_x^h - 0.5 \cdot \lambda + \mu^{hj} \cdot U_x^h - \mu^{jh} \cdot U_x^{jh} = 0$$

$$\frac{\partial F}{\partial I^h} = 0.5 \cdot u_I^h + 0.5 \cdot \lambda + \mu^{hj} \cdot u_I^h - \mu^{jh} \cdot u_I^{jh} = 0$$

$$\frac{\partial F}{\partial z} = 0.5 \cdot \left[U_z^1 + U_z^2\right] - \lambda \cdot wL_z^z + \mu^{12} \cdot \left[U_z^1 - U_z^{12}\right] + \mu^{21} \cdot \left[U_z^2 - U_z^{21}\right] = 0, \tag{7.9}$$

where $h \neq j = 1, 2, L_z^z = \partial L^z/\partial z$, and $U_1^h < 0$ (because it reflects the marginal utility cost of supplying labor). However, we must also account for the self-selection constraints:

$$\frac{\partial F}{\partial \mu^{12}} = U^1\left(x^1,z\right) + u^1\left(I^1\right) - U^1\left(x^2,z\right) - u^1\left(I^2\right) \geq 0;$$

$$\mu^{12} \geq 0; \quad \mu^{12} \cdot \frac{\partial F}{\partial \mu^{12}} = 0$$

$$\frac{\partial F}{\partial \mu^{21}} = U^2\left(x^2, z\right) + u^2\left(l^2\right) - U^2\left(x^1, z\right) - u^2\left(l^1\right) \geq 0;$$

$$\mu^{21} \geq 0; \quad \mu^{21} \cdot \frac{\partial F}{\partial \mu^{21}} = 0. \tag{7.9'}$$

These conditions are stated here as Karush-Kuhn-Tucker conditions, allowing for corner solutions. To keep the presentation as simple as possible, let us focus on the case where agents gain from selecting the allocation intended for them. In this (first-best) case, the two Lagrange multipliers μ^{12} and μ^{21} must equal zero because agents should gain from selecting the allocation intended for them, i.e., $\partial F/\partial \mu^{hj} > 0$ for $h \neq j = 1, 2$. From (7.9), it follows that, at the optimum, the marginal utility of consumption of the private good equals the negative of the marginal disutility of work effort. Moreover, they are the same for both types of agents. In addition, drawing on Sandmo (1998), it follows from the final line in (7.9) that converting the expression from units of utility to monetary units by division by $0.5 \cdot \left(U_x^1 + U_x^2\right)$, i.e., by the average private marginal utility of income as captured by U_x^h, implies that the MCPF equals one. Hence, this case reduces to Samuelson's (1954) rule for the optimal public good provision. A good graphical illustration of this case is found in Boadway and Keen (1993).

Gahvari (2006, p. 1259) shows that:

$$MCPF^{Ga} \underset{<}{\overset{>}{=}} 1 \Leftrightarrow \sum_h \sum_{j \neq h} \mu^{hj} \cdot \left(U_x^h - U_x^{hj}\right) \underset{<}{\overset{>}{=}} 0. \tag{7.10}$$

Thus, if optimal income taxation is available in the multi-agent case, then $\mu^{hj} = 0$ for all h, implying that the MCPF equals one. If optimal income taxation is not available, a subset of μ^{hj}'s must be strictly positive. Whether MCPF exceeds or falls short of one depends on the sign of the Lagrange multiplier multiplied by the difference between the marginal utility of consumption if selecting the intended allocation and selecting the j-type agent's allocation. MCPF will exceed (fall short of) one if the sum across agents is strictly positive (negative). Refer to Gahvari (2006, pp. 1259–61) for further details of this quite involved case.

However, the tax structure in the considered model is extremely simple. In reality, there are many different types of taxes: income taxes, commodity taxes, value-added taxes, capital taxes, property taxes, and so on. Diamond (1998) uses a variation of the Mirrlees model to show that under certain conditions, marginal tax rates should be rising at high-income levels and declining in an interval containing the modal skill. Diamond and Saez (2011) argue that very high earners should be subject to high and rising marginal tax rates on earnings, while the earnings of low-income families should be subsidized, and those subsidies should then be phased out with high implicit marginal tax rates. They also argue that capital income should be taxed. These considerations seem to suggest that the MCPF could be quite high. Piketty and Saez (2013) provide, among other things, a historical review of labor income taxation.

On the other hand, Christiansen (2007) claims that if a sufficiently rich tax regime exists, one could rely on the Pareto criterion, which would be less information-demanding than a social welfare approach requiring access to social welfare weights assigned to various groups. He also argues that – whatever the available tax regime – CBA runs into problems unless one can assume that taxes are set optimally. Jacobs (2018) forcefully argues that the SMCPF is equal to one (and the Dutch government has followed his advice). Instead, there are distributional characteristics affecting both benefits and costs. In addition, Jacobs (2018, p. 906) assumes that lump-sum taxation is the marginal source of public finance. As discussed in Subsubsection 3.4 his approach is problematic. Holtsmark (2019) has criticized Jacobs, and claims that there is a weak basis for the conclusion that the optimal MCPF equals one; basically, Holtsmark applies another definition of the MCPF by converting units of utility to monetary units by dividing $1 + t$. Bos et al. (2019) argue that the MCPF should be set equal to one; the marginal distributional benefits of taxation are equal to the marginal distortionary effects of taxation. However, they have been heavily criticized by Boardman et al. (2020). According to Gahvari (2006, p. 1252), Kaplow (1996, 2004) argues that if a distribution-neutral income tax adjustment is employed, labor supply and distributional concerns should play no role in decisions regarding the provision of a public good. Instead, simply compare the marginal rate of transformation and the sum of individuals' marginal rates of substitution between public and private goods. Thus, there are indeed mixed views on the likely magnitude of the MCPF when distributional issues are involved.

There is also an alternative approach to the optimal provision of public goods, arguing that distributional concerns are irrelevant to the evaluation of public projects. This line of research holds that the income tax can undo unintended distributional effects. The approach relies on the benefit principle, which, building on the flexibility of the nonlinear income tax, argues that each individual should contribute to financing a public good corresponding to her marginal willingness to pay. A good reference to this approach is Kreiner and Verdelin (2012). By adjusting the nonlinear income tax, they show that the simple Samuelson rule is reinvigorated when preferences are separable in goods and leisure. This approach is not further considered in this Element because it seems hard to implement.

8 A Few Reflections on Empirical Approaches

This final section reflects on the empirical estimates of the MCPF, focusing on recent literature. Empirical studies on the MCPF employ a variety of methods, including CGE models, microsimulation models, and econometric approaches. There are also partial equilibrium simulation methods. We begin by giving a few examples of these methods and then discuss ways to obtain MCPF using the theory outlined in this Element.

Barrios et al. (2013) compare wage taxes and green taxes using a CGE model, the GEM-E3 model, covering 24 EU countries and the rest of the world. Later versions include 38 countries/regions where all EU member states and the most significant economies globally (USA, China, Brazil, Russia, Canada, India, and so on) are individually represented. In their equation (3), they estimate what appears to be a discrete or non-marginal variation of EV/S. As argued in Subsection 4.4, this seems to result in an estimate of something else than the MCPF. Elgin et al. (2022) build a dynamic general equilibrium model with formal and informal sectors and allow the government to use consumption, capital, and labor income taxes to raise revenue. They use data from 2010 and cover 45 countries across different regions. Dixon et al. (2012) evaluate MCPF for different tax types in Finland using the VATTAGE model, a dynamic applied general equilibrium framework. They find that MCPF is lowest for income tax increases and highest for VAT increases, highlighting income taxes as the most efficient revenue source. The MCPF for the entire tax package rises over time, reaching approximately 1.5 in the long run, signaling significant societal costs of additional tax revenues. The broadcasting tax shows intermediate efficiency, balancing revenue generation with lower distortions compared to VAT. As discussed in Subsection 6.2 of this Element, using time-dependent MCPFs could potentially introduce a time-dependency problem. This suggests that evaluators should use a constant present value MCPF to avoid a "policy-decision problem." Sørensen (2014) uses a general equilibrium model with labor and capital to estimate the marginal deadweight loss from taxation in a small open economy. The framework accounts for interactions among the major tax bases and allows a decomposition of the deadweight loss into the losses arising from the shrinkage of each tax base. The quite ambitious approach was applied to estimate the marginal deadweight loss from major tax instruments in Sweden. However, applying the approach to 27 EU countries and the rest of the world is probably both time and resource-consuming. Beaud (2008) estimates the MCPF in France using a general equilibrium model incorporating household consumption and labor supply data. By calibrating the model with data from the 2001 Budget des Familles survey and France's tax codes, it calculates

MCPFs for various tax reforms. The results show MCPFs ranging from 0.95 to 2.16, with income tax reforms targeting high-income brackets having the highest values due to labor supply distortions. Lump-sum taxes and VAT reforms yield lower MCPFs, particularly for reduced VAT rates, as they create fewer economic distortions. We will comment on the finding that MCPF is less than one on the following page.

Microsimulation models provide a detailed perspective by focusing on the effects of tax policies at the household level, abstracting from market repercussions. Figari et al. (2018) use the Italian component of EUROMOD, a European-wide tax-benefit microsimulation model, to estimate MCPFs. This model displays distributional impacts of tax policies, revealing how different income groups bear the burden of taxation. They study effects of labor taxes (including social security) on both the intensive (number of hours worked by individuals who are already employed) and extensive margin (changes in the number of individuals who are employed), i.e. the entry and exit decisions. In this type of model, the agent decides whether it is worthwhile to enter the labor market and, conditional on entering, the number of hours to work. Incorporating the entry cost causes a considerable increase in the MCPF. The reason is that an income tax hike increases the entry cost and hence reduces the number of households entering the job market. Bessho and Hayashi (2013) use a microdata approach to estimate individual MCPFs. These can be aggregated to estimate the (Japanese) economy's MCPF. After elaborating on aspects of distributional weights, they estimate the wage elasticity of labor supply and the individual MCPFs on a household basis.

There is also a kind an intermediate approach used by Campbell and Bond (1997). The authors use a calibrated partial equilibrium model to estimate the MCPF in Australia. They analyze labor supply responses to a simulated 1% increase in marginal tax rates across income deciles, using data from the 1988-89 Household Expenditure Survey. By calibrating the model with effective marginal and average tax rates and labor supply elasticities, they calculate how taxation distorts labor supply and generates deadweight loss. The iterative simulation adjusts for both substitution effects (reduced labor due to lower after-tax wages) and income effects (potential increased labor to offset lost income), converging to a new equilibrium for labor supply and tax revenue. The MCPF is then computed as the ratio of the total social cost of raising revenue (including deadweight loss) to the nominal tax revenue raised, yielding values between 1.19 and 1.24 depending on labor supply elasticities.

Turning to econometric approaches, Dahlby and Ferede (2012, 2018) find relatively high estimates of the MCPF for Canadian provinces. Kleven and Kreiner (2006) estimate the MCPF for 15 European countries by incorporating labor market entry and exit decisions, similar to Figare et al. (2018). An earlier study by Kleven and Kreiner (2003) extends this analysis to all OECD countries, providing a broader view of labor market participation and its sensitivity to tax policies.

It is hardly surprising that there are differences between the approaches. For example, the measures estimated by Barrios et al. (2013) are non-marginal measures that capture all general equilibrium adjustments in prices and so on caused by the change in the tax rate. In any case, using, for example, (4.10') and later versions of the GEM-E3 model could provide a quick and cheap way of approximating the MCPF for EU countries and the rest of the world. The results by Barrios et al. (2013) suggest that there exist tax sources that generate MCPFs that are close to unity for the EU countries. MCPFs Indeed, Bjertnaes (2015) claims that if one accounts for transfers to low-income non-entrants, the MCPF is close to unity. Similarly, Christiansen (2007) argues that there are theoretical reasons why the MCPF should be equal to one. And, as we have seen, the Mirrlees type of approach, discussed in Section 7, implies that the MCPF could equal one.

On the surface, it would seem possible to go further and argue that *MCPF* could be less than one if externalities are involved (and we also saw this possibility in the Beaud (2008) study already discussed, which did not involve externalities). For example, a green tax may cause a decrease in emissions and such a tax is not distortive, rather corrective. See Subsection 5.3 and Subsection A.3 of the Appendix for details. However, if energy is a non-Giffen commodity, the MEB plus one should result in an MCPF that exceeds one. Similarly, equation (5.10) in the current Element, with the expression within parenthesis in the numerator of MCPF equal to unity, suggests that MCPF > 1. Again, a non-marginal numerical general equilibrium approach might produce a different result. On the surface, equation (3) in Barrios et al. (2013) is such an example. It captures a discrete or non-marginal EV over the estimated change in tax revenue, i.e., *EV/S*. But this is an approximation of EB rather than MCPF.

The approach typically employed in major manuals is to set the MCPF (explicitly or implicitly) to one. Examples are provided by the European Commission. (2014), the European Investment Bank (2023), HM Treasury (2011, 2022), and the US EPA. (2010).

Let us now discuss empirical approaches using the methodology outlined in this Element. One possibility is to draw on a variation of equation (4.10) in Subsection 4.4. For convenient reference, the equation is repeated here:

$$\frac{dEV}{dS} = \frac{1}{1 - \frac{t_w \cdot w}{L^s} \frac{\partial L^s}{\partial w_d}} = MCPF^{t_w}. \tag{4.10'}$$

A possible and simple estimation approach is as follows. Interpret x^d as an aggregate (nondurable) composite consumption commodity, i.e., as a proxy for real (nondurable) private consumption, and t as the average tax rate on private consumption. If one can find price and income/expenditure elasticities for real private consumption (or aggregate across commodity groups), a simple estimate of the MCPF is obtained. Either as equation (3.4) but with $t_w = 0$ (or adding an estimate of the labor elasticity when $t_w > 0$) or as equation (4.1).

Labor supply elasticities and labor taxes as a share of GDP can be found in Barrios et al. (2013); see their Tables 1 and 6.[23] This allows a rough approximation of equation (4.10'). It might be noted that (4.10') results in MCPFs that are much closer to one than those reported in Barrios et al. (2013), at least for a tiny sample of countries.

Another suggestion, valid for a small project evaluated at its optimum, is to use the ratio of the marginal present value benefits and the direct present value project costs as a measure of the MCPF. However, this approach does not work for a non-marginal project. Consider equation (4.1), and suppose that we somehow can solve t, V_m, L^z, and w (and possibly p) as functions of z. Then, one can integrate equation (A.6) from z^0 to z^1, where a superscript 0 (1) refers to the initial (final) level of provision of the public good. This is a definite integral; compare Johansson (2021). However, it is not possible to "factor out" or separate the direct project cost from the MCPF. Another problem with using the ratio (for a small project) is that the ratio is sensitive to the classification of items as benefits or negative costs. To illustrate, suppose benefits are equal to 10 +20 and that the direct cost equals 25; the MCPF is estimated to be 6/5. Next, suppose that benefits equal to 20 are classified as negative costs. Then, the ratio is 10/(25–20), suggesting that the MCPF equals 2. Note that the difference between benefits and costs is equal to 5 in both considered cases. Moreover, as is well-known, using Marshallian concepts to evaluate large changes is questionable. The preferred approach is to switch to Hicksian or income-compensated concepts.

Society undertakes a huge number of different projects every year. These can be assumed to be financed by raising one or more taxes. Most commodity and income taxes are associated with MCPFs that exceed one. However, "green taxes" that reduce climate change might be associated with low MCPFs (as is numerically illustrated in Subsection A.3 of the Appendix). If such green taxes

---

[23] Note that their Table 1 adds social security fees to labor taxes. This is a questionable procedure because these fees are returned to employees as pensions, sickness benefits, and so on. See also Bjertnaes (2015). It seems unclear how Barrios et al. have estimated the MCPFs for the green tax; seemingly, no price elasticities are provided.

become more and more common, it might not seem unreasonable to set MCPF equal to one for a typical project, a kind of Arrow and Lind (1970) argument.

A final approach that could be considered is to undertake a base-case economic evaluation and add a risk analysis or stochastic sensitivity analysis. Key parameters are attributed (truncated) distributions, such as normal or uniform, or triangular ones. The outcome could be summarized in a survival/survivor function. This function provides the estimated probability that the investment generates a specific outcome or better, for example, at least breaks even. A recent application for a "green" investment is provided by Johansson and Kriström (2022). It should be possible to develop a simple Excel-based tool kit that allows investigators to insert a number of parameter values and then obtain the survivor function.

Appendix

A.1 The Basic Utility Maximization Problem

Consider the utility maximization behind the indirect utility function in equation (3.1). Assume there are H identical agents. Each agent is equipped with a well-behaved direct utility function:

$$U = U(z, x, x^{nu}, \text{TE} - L), \tag{A.1}$$

where z denotes the public good, which can be simultaneously consumed by all agents, x and x^{nu} are private goods, TE denotes the time endowment, and L denotes working time, i.e., $\text{TE} - L$ equals leisure time. This function is maximized subject to a budget constraint:

$$\pi - T + (1 - t_w) \cdot w \cdot L - (p + t) \cdot x - 1 \cdot x^{nu} = 0, \tag{A.2}$$

where π denotes any profit income, treated as a lump-sum income by the agent, T denotes a lump-sum tax (say, a property tax), $w_d = (1 - t_w) \cdot w$ denotes the after-tax wage, and $q = p + t$ denotes the consumer price of x. Thus, there are three different taxes: a lump-sum tax T, a unit commodity tax t, and a proportional wage tax t_w. If the profit income is absent or insufficient to cover T, then the deficit is covered by paying with money from the labor income.

Suppose that there were no taxes initially in equation (A.2). Then, one could multiply all three prices by a common tax factor $(1 + t^c) > 1$. This would be equivalent to lump-sum taxation, where the lump-sum income is multiplied by $1/(1 + t^c)$, i.e., there is no EB or deadweight of taxation. Note that this subsidizes labor (because labor appears with a plus sign) but implies that leisure is implicitly taxed. Without lump-sum income, the approach would result in zero tax revenue. Thus, taxing the two goods is equivalent to taxing labor. This justifies the tax regime applied in this Element, where we want to tax a good and labor. Refer to Auerbach and Hines (2002, pp. 1362–65) for details.

The Lagrangian associated with this maximization problem can be stated as follows:

$$F(.) = U(z, x, x^{nu}, \text{TE} - L) + v \cdot (\pi - T + w_d \cdot L - q \cdot x - 1 \cdot x^{nu}), \tag{A.3}$$

where v denotes a Lagrange multiplier. Solving the maximization problem and summing across agents yields the Utilitarian social welfare function:

$$H \cdot V = H \cdot V(z, q, w_d, \pi - T). \tag{A.4}$$

Taken together the agents are willing to pay $H \cdot V_z/V_m dz$ for a small or marginal increase in the provision of the public good, where V_m converts the marginal utility V_z provided by the public good to a willingness to pay for *dz* additional units of the good. However, to avoid clutter, multiply through equation (A.4) by $1/H$. Then, we arrive at the indirect utility function in equation (3.1) in Section 3.2. Note that the marginal utility of income V_m is equal to the Lagrange multiplier v associated with the agent's budget constraint in equation (A.3); $\partial F/\partial m = v$ with $m = \pi - T$. This is important to realize when lump-sum taxation is not available or $m = 0$. Using equation (A.3), a small ceteris paribus increase in the commodity tax is seen to cause a welfare loss equal to $\partial F/\partial t = -v \cdot x^d$, while a marginal increase in the labor tax reduces welfare by $\partial F/\partial t_w = -v \cdot w \cdot L^s$, where a superscript is added to signal that a derivative is evaluated at an optimum. A small increase in the provision of the public good causes welfare to increase by $\partial F/\partial z = U_z$.

The envelope theorem asserts that the *partial* derivative of the Lagrange function (A.3) with respect to a parameter is equal to the corresponding *total* derivative. The latter derivative is obtained by totally differentiating the Lagrangian with respect to the parameter. For example, the middle line in equation (3.6), covering the partial derivative of the Lagrangian with respect to z, is equal to the total derivative with respect to z (and is set equal to zero in the equation to obtain the optimal provision of the public good). For details, refer to Johansson and Kriström (2016, pp. 10–11) and Florio (2014, pp. 84–88) or any textbook on advanced microeconomics.

Equation (3.6) assumes that preferences are weakly separable in the public good and other goods. Without this assumption, one has to add $\lambda \cdot (t\partial x^d/\partial z + t_w \cdot w\partial L^s/\partial z)\, dz$ to the benefits in the middle line in (3.6) and to $\partial F/\partial z$ if (A.3) is evaluated, provided $t, t_w > 0$. It seems to be an open question if this expression adds to or deducts from the project's primary benefits. For example, if the public good and the private one are substitutes (in the sense that $\partial x^d/\partial z < 0$) and more of the public good induces the agent to spend less time working, then the term is negative. The reverse outcome is also a possibility. In any case, it seems extremely difficult to estimate the two derivatives. How does the output of a new project affect the demand for the private good and the supply of labor? In a multi-agent context, one can define distributional characteristics, see Subsection 7.1, based on covariances, but they, too, seem hard to estimate. Simple MCPF formulas, on the other hand, seem reasonably straightforward to estimate.

A.2 A Numerical and Graphical Illustration of the MCPF versus MEB

The difference between MCPF and the EB can be illuminated using a simple logarithmic Cobb-Douglas indirect utility function, where the agent has a lump-sum income but no endogenous wage income:

$$V(.) = \ln\left(\frac{m}{2 \cdot q}\right) + \ln\left(\frac{m}{2 \cdot 1}\right), \tag{A.5}$$

where $q = p + t$, p is kept constant, the expressions within parentheses are demand functions, and the second commodity acts as numéraire whose price is set equal to one. Thus, a commodity tax is used to illustrate any difference between the MCPF and the EB. Consider now the EV that makes the agent as well off as with an increase in the commodity tax from t^1 to t^2, changing the end-user price from q^1 to q^2:

$$\ln\left(\frac{m + EV}{2 \cdot q^1}\right) + \ln\left(\frac{m + EV}{2}\right) = \ln\left(\frac{m}{2 \cdot q^2}\right) + \ln\left(\frac{m}{2}\right), \tag{A.6}$$

where EV denotes the equivalent variation, a payment that keeps the agent at the same (lower) utility level as with the increase in the tax.[1] It can be shown that $EV = m \cdot \left(\sqrt{q^1/q^2} - 1\right)$. Thus, EV < 0, i.e., a payment to avoid the tax increase when $q^2 > q^1$. It corresponds to the area to the left of a compensated or Hicksian demand curve between the two prices; compare Figure A.1, which also illustrates the associated EB. For a small price increase, it can be approximated by the area to the left of the ordinary or Marshallian demand curve in Figure 1 between q^1 and q^2.

The change in tax revenue equals $\Delta S = m \cdot \left[t^2/(2 \cdot q^2) - t^1/(2 \cdot q^1)\right]$. Consider now the ratio between the negative of EV and ΔS:

$$-\frac{EV}{\Delta S} = -\frac{\left(\sqrt{q^1/q^2} - 1\right)}{t^2/(2 \cdot q^2) - t^1/(2 \cdot q^1)}. \tag{A.7}$$

If the expression is evaluated as t^2 approaches t^1, one obtains $0/0$. However, applying l'Hôpital's rule, i.e., differentiating the numerator and the denominator separately with respect to t^1, and evaluating the ratio at $t^2 = t^1$, i.e., at $q^2 = q^1$, yields:[2]

$$\lim_{q^2 \to q^1} \frac{\dfrac{q^1}{2 \cdot \sqrt{q^1/q^2} \cdot (q^2)^2}}{\dfrac{1}{2 \cdot q^2}\left(1 - \dfrac{t^2}{q^2}\right)} = \frac{\dfrac{q^1}{q^2}}{1 - \dfrac{t^2}{q^2}} = \frac{q^1}{p} \tag{A.8}$$

where the first upper ratio refers to the derivative of the negative of EV and the lower one to the derivative of ΔS.

---

[1] Thus, the sign convention applied here is such that the agent would need compensation in terms of the CV if $t^2 > t^1$.

[2] For more on l'Hôpital's rule, see, for example, page 481 in Varian (1992) or Section 8.8.3 in Johansson and Kriström (2016).

Based on equation (4.1) the marginal cost of public funds equals:

$$MCPF^t = \frac{1}{1 - t^1/(p + t^1)} = \frac{q^1}{p}. \tag{A.9}$$

Thus, in the limit, (A.8) equals $MCPF^t$.[3] Moreover, (A.8) and (A.9) are equal to one if $t^1 = 0$ and exceed one if $t^1 > 0$. However, not even in this extremely simple model will they coincide if the change in the tax rate is discrete or non-marginal. Integrating equation (4.1) for a large change in the provision of the public good but holding utility constant provides a CBA of a non-marginal project, where the MCPF plays an important role. Although an essential welfare-economic concept, the MEB seems to play no obvious role in project appraisal. In particular, using equation (A.7) to approximate the MCPF when the evaluated changes are non-marginal seems strange, to say the least. Making the changes smaller and smaller causes the measure to approach 0/0.

Given a non-marginal increase in a commodity tax, the EB is illustrated in Figure A.1. Initially, there is no tax on the commodity and the equilibrium configuration is q^0, x^0. After introducing a unit tax, the equilibrium occurs at q^1, x^1. The tax revenue equals $\Delta q \cdot x^1$, assuming that the producer price remains

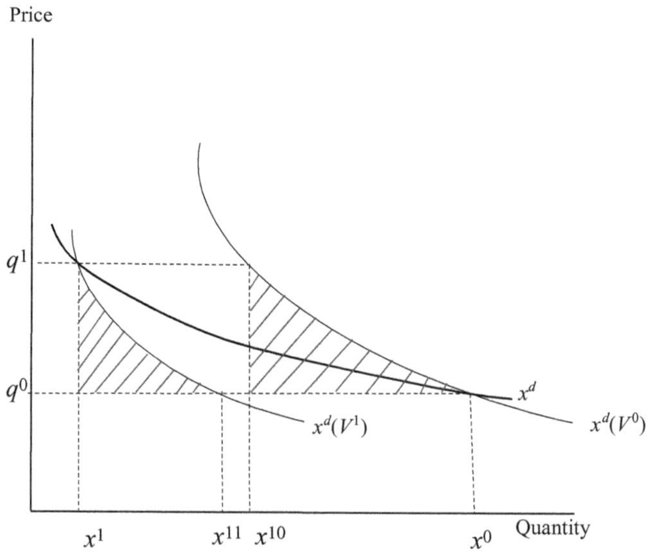

Figure A.1 Illustration of the excess burden

---

[3] Alternatively, the result can be obtained by taking the partial derivative of EV with respect to q^2. Evaluate the expression at $q^2 = q^1$ and divide by the change in tax revenue evaluated at $t^2 = t^1$.

constant. In addition to the ordinary or Marshallian demand curve, denoted x^d, two compensated or Hicksian demand curves are in the figure. The outer keeps the agent at her initial or pre-tax utility level, V^0. The inner one keeps the agent at her final, lower, utility level, V^1. The CV is given by the area to the left of the outer curve between the two prices. The EV equals the area to the left of the inner curve between q^0 and q^1. In this case, EV is the maximal payment the agent is willing to make to avoid the tax increase, while CV is the smallest compensation the agent needs in order to remain at the pre-tax level of utility.

The EB can be defined for each of the two compensated concepts by deducting the relevant tax revenue from EV and CV, respectively. The EB associated with the inner curve is equal to the dashed triangular area under the curve between Δq and x^{11} and x^1. $\Delta q \cdot x^{10}$ gives the tax revenue associated with the outer curve. Hence, the EB equals the dashed triangular area under the curve between Δq and x^0 and x^{10}. It is seen that an EB referring to the uncompensated demand curve cannot be given an interpretation in terms of WTP or WTA, in general. However, it could provide an acceptable approximation for very small tax increases. Willig (1976) provides reasonable bounds for approximating CV and EV with the ordinary consumer surplus.

In terms of the numerical example based on equation (A.6), the EB equals $-EV - \Delta S$. Dividing by the additional tax revenue ΔS yields the EB per euro of tax revenue.

According to Auerbach and Hines (2002, p. 1386) "the deadweight loss of a tax system and the MCPF are two entirely separate concepts. Deadweight loss is a measure of the potential gain from replacing distortionary taxes with an efficient lump-sum alternative, and marginal deadweight loss is simply the change in this magnitude as tax revenue changes. By contrast, the MCPF reflects the welfare cost, in units of a numéraire commodity, of raising tax revenue for exhaustive government expenditure." However, as demonstrated in Section 4.4, EB + 1 (= MEB + 1) equals MCPF in the limit.

A.3 A Tax on Emissions

In Subsection 5.3 a case is considered where a tax on emissions finances a project. In the case where both private sector demand for goods and the provision of the public good causes emissions, the Lagrangian is as follows:

$$F(.) = V\left[z, q, w_d, m, g\left[c\left(x^d + z\right)\right]\right] + \lambda \cdot \left((t + t_{Em}) \cdot x^d - w \cdot L^d\right), \quad (A.10)$$

where $q = p + t + t_{Em}$, c denotes an emission conversion factor, for simplicity set equal to one, and the function $g(.)$ denotes the total damage caused by harmful emissions. The partial derivative of g with respect to x^d is denoted g_x and is positive, i.e., the total damage increases if x^d and/or z increases. First-order conditions for an interior solution include:

$$\frac{\partial F}{\partial t_{Em}} = -V_m \cdot x^d + V_{Em} g_x \frac{\partial x^d}{\partial q} + \lambda \cdot x^d \cdot \left(1 + \frac{(t + t_{Em})}{x^d} \frac{\partial x^d}{\partial q}\right) = 0$$

$$\frac{\partial F}{\partial z} = V_z + V_{Em} g_x - \lambda \cdot w \frac{\partial L^z}{\partial z} = 0, \tag{A.11}$$

where subscripts refer to partial derivatives. After some calculations, one arrives at the following MCPF:

$$\frac{\lambda}{V_m} = \left(1 - \frac{V_{Em}}{x^d} g_x \frac{\partial x^d}{\partial q}\right) \frac{1}{1 + \frac{(t+t_{Em})}{x^d} \frac{\partial x^d}{\partial q}}. \tag{A.12}$$

Multiplying through the final line of (A.11) by $(1/V_m)\,dz$ and inserting (A.12) yields the following cost–benefit rule:

$$\frac{V_z}{V_m} dz - w dL^z \left(1 - \frac{V_{Em}}{x^d} g_x \frac{\partial x^d}{\partial q}\right) \frac{1}{1 + \frac{t}{x^d} \frac{\partial x^d}{\partial q}} + \frac{V_{Em}}{V_m} g_x dz = 0. \tag{A.13}$$

This replicates the rule discussed in Section 5.3.

A numerical illustration of this result is added. A logarithmic Cobb-Douglas utility function is augmented by a quadratic function representing an environmental impact, however measured, caused by demands for goods; $g(.) = \left(0.1 \cdot [x^d + z]\right)^2$, where 0.1 is the constant emission conversion factor. Thus, damage is increasing at an increasing rate in the magnitude of $x^d + z$. For simplicity, the impact is converted to welfare units at a constant rate (equal to 0.1). Hence, the utility function is as follows:

$$U = \ln(z) + \ln\left[x^d\right] + \ln\left[x^{nu}\right] + \ln\left[\mathrm{TE} - L^s\right] - 0.1 \cdot \left(0.1 \cdot \left[x^d + z\right]\right)^2, \tag{A.14}$$

where x^{nu} denotes the untaxed numéraire, TE denotes the time endowment, and $\partial U/\partial g = -0.1$. The demand and supply functions are as follows:

$$x^d = (m + \mathrm{TE} \cdot w_d)/(3 \cdot q); \; x^n u = (m + \mathrm{TE} \cdot w)/(3 \cdot 1); \; L^s = (-m + 2 \cdot \mathrm{TE} \cdot w)/(3 \cdot w)$$

where $m = 1$, $q = 1 + t_{Em}$, $w_d = w = 5$, and $\mathrm{TE} = 24$. Hence, the indirect utility function equals:

$$V = \ln(z) + \ln\left[\frac{m + \mathrm{TE} \cdot w_d}{3 \cdot q}\right] + \ln\left[\frac{(m + \mathrm{TE} \cdot w_d)}{3 \cdot 1}\right]$$

$$+ \ln\left[\mathrm{TE} - \left(\frac{-m + 2 \cdot \mathrm{TE} \cdot w_d}{3 \cdot w_d}\right)\right] - 0.1 \cdot \left(0.1 \cdot \left[x^d + z\right]\right)^2 \tag{A.15}$$

The Lagrangian for this simple problem is as follows:

$$F = V(.) + \lambda \cdot \left(t_{Em} \cdot x^d - w \cdot z^2\right), \tag{A.16}$$

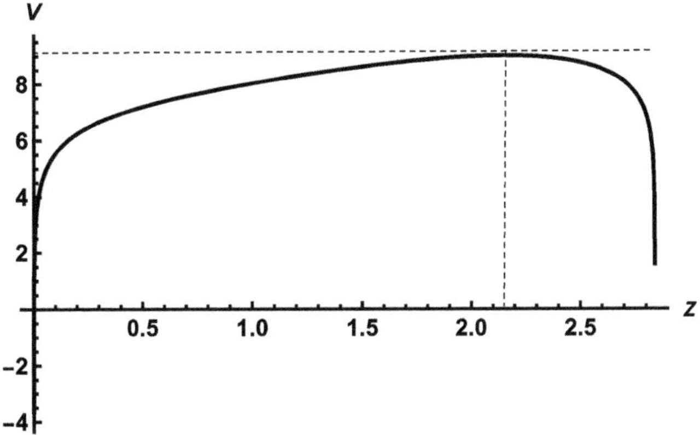

Figure A.2 Social welfare as a function of z when $10^{-5} \leq z \leq 2.84$

where the public sector's production function equals $z = (L^z)^{1/2}$, and only private consumption is taxed. Note that the government's budget constraint implies that $t_{Em} \to \infty$ as z goes to around 2.8401877872 and then becomes negative, implying that V becomes a complex number, i.e., then involves an imaginary part. Thus, add the constraint $0 < z \leq 2.84$. First-order conditions for an interior solution are $\partial F/\partial t_{em} = \partial F/\partial z = \partial F/\partial \lambda = 0$. The suggested optimal values are $t_{Em} \approx 1.353$, $z \approx 2.154$, and $\lambda \approx 0.02$. The suggested solution can be shown to be a saddle point of the Lagrangian and hence a global maximum of $V(.)$ according to the Saddle Point Theorem; see, for example, Boyd and Vandenberghe (2004, Ch. 5). It also fulfills conventional criteria for a local optimum as stated in, for example, Jehle and Reny (2011, pp. 588–90) or Varian (1992, pp. 498–501). Refer also to Figure A.2.

Drawing on equation (A.11), the first-order condition for the optimal provision of z, but ignoring emissions caused by the project, and after division by V_m, equals:

$$\frac{dV/dz}{V_m} = \frac{1}{z}\frac{1}{V_m} - 2 \cdot w \cdot z \cdot \frac{\lambda}{V_m} \approx 1.556, \tag{A.17}$$

where $V_m = 3/121$. This suggests that the provision of the good should be increased. However, drawing on equations (A.11) and (A.15), the environmental cost caused by the added provision of z equals $0.002 \cdot (121/(3 \cdot (1 + t_{em})) + z)/V_m \approx 1.556$ at the optimum. This cost should be deducted from (A.17), illustrating that $z \approx 2.154$ represents an optimum. Recall that the total expression should equal zero at an interior optimum. Moreover, the conventional definition of MCPF $= \lambda/V_m$ is equal to about 0.8, i.e., below one, while z is seemingly too small. However, the latter reflects the fact that the project itself causes emissions.

Finally, a graphical illustration is added. Use the government's budget constraint to obtain t_{Em} as a function of z; $t_{Em} = 15z^2/(15z^2 - 121)$. The relationship between welfare and z is captured by the curve in Figure A.2, which can be shown to reach a maximum at $z \approx 2.154$.

A.4 A Private-Sector Project

Subsection 5.5 introduces a private-sector project. The Lagrangian is as follows:

$$F(.) = V\left[z, q, w_d, \pi + p \cdot x^N - w \cdot L^N\left(x^N\right)\right] + \lambda \cdot \left(t \cdot x^d - w \cdot L^z\right), \qquad (A.18)$$

where $T = t_w = 0$, and a superscript N refers to the new firm entering the market. First-order conditions for an interior solution include:

$$\frac{\partial F}{\partial t} = -V_m x^d + \lambda \cdot x^d \cdot \left(1 + \frac{t}{x^d}\frac{\partial x^d}{\partial q}\right) = 0$$

$$\frac{\partial F}{\partial x^N} = V_m \cdot \left(p - w\frac{\partial L^N}{\partial x^N}\right) + \lambda \cdot t\frac{\partial x^d}{\partial m}\left(p - w\frac{\partial L^N}{\partial x^N}\right) = 0. \qquad (A.19)$$

The final term in the second line appears because profit income is an argument in the demand function. The condition for the optimal public good provision is suppressed in the current case because the focus is on the private commodity. Using the first line in (A.19), straightforward calculations reveal that:

$$\frac{\lambda}{V_m} = \frac{1}{1 + \frac{t}{x^d}\frac{\partial x^d}{\partial q}}. \qquad (A.20)$$

This is the familiar multiplier. Using (A.20) in the final line of (A.19), one obtains:

$$\left(p - w\frac{\partial L^N}{\partial x^N}\right) \cdot \left[1 + t\frac{\partial x^d}{\partial m} \cdot \frac{\lambda}{V_m}\right] = 0. \qquad (A.21)$$

This replicates equation (5.20), but note that (A.21) cannot equal zero unless the firm maximizes profits, i.e., produces an amount such that $p = w\partial L^N/\partial x^N$. A closer inspection of (A.19) reveals that both conditions for an interior solution where $x^N > 0$ cannot be satisfied simultaneously unless the firm maximizes profits.

A.5 Endogenous Wage Rate

The indirect utility function is stated as follows:

$$V = (z, q, (w \cdot (1 - t_w), m) = V(z, q, w_d, m) , \tag{A.22}$$

where $m = \pi(.) = \pi^d + \pi^{nu}$. Hence, we rule out lump-sum taxation.

Consider now a marginal increase in the provision of the public good financed by the tax on labor:

$$\begin{aligned}
\frac{dV}{V_m} &= \frac{V_z}{V_m} dz + L^s \cdot [(1 - t_w) \, dw - w dt_w] - L dw \\
&= \frac{V_z}{V_m} dz - L^s \cdot (t_w dw + w dt_w) + L^z dw, \tag{A.23}
\end{aligned}$$

where $L = L^d + L^{nu}$, L^s equals $L + L^z$ in equilibrium, and $q = p$ is assumed to remain constant. The final term in the middle expression reflects the change in aggregate profit income as the market wage adjusts; $\partial \pi / \partial w = - L$. The final term on the right-hand side is added because it was deducted to obtain $(L^s - L - L^z) \, dw = 0$.

Use the government's budget constraint $t_w \cdot w \cdot L^s = w \cdot L^z$ to determine how the budget is affected by the increase in z and t_w:

$$w dL^z + L^z dw = w \cdot L^s dt_w + t_w \cdot L^s dw + t_w \cdot w \frac{dL^s}{\partial w_d}[(1 - t_w) \, dw - w dt_w \,)]$$

$$- t_w w \frac{\partial L^s}{\partial m} L dw = L^s \cdot (t_w dw + w dt_w) - t_w \cdot w \frac{\partial L^s}{\partial w_d}(t_w dw + w dt_w)$$

$$+ t_w \cdot w \frac{\partial L^{sH}}{\partial w_d} dw + t_w \cdot w \frac{\partial L^s}{\partial m} L^z dw = L^s \cdot (t_w dw + w dt_w) \cdot$$

$$\left[1 - \frac{t_w \cdot w}{L^s} \frac{\partial L^s}{\partial w_d} + \frac{t_w \cdot w}{L^s \cdot (t_w dw + w dt_w)} \left(\frac{\partial L^{sH}}{\partial w_d} + \frac{\partial L^s}{\partial m} L^z\right) dw\right], \tag{A.24}$$

where $\partial L^s / \partial w_d$ contains both a substitution effect and an income effect. The latter effect is "netted out" against the income effect in the final term in the first line. Hence, there is a Hicksian or income-compensated supply function in the final line indicated by a superscript H. However, if $L^z > 0$, then there remains an income effect, as reflected by the final term within parentheses.

Next, use (A.24) in (A.23) and multiply the denominator by w_d / w_d. Then, the MCPF can be expressed in terms of supply elasticities, and the evaluation rule becomes:

$$\frac{dV}{V_m} = \frac{V_z}{V_m} dz - (w dL^z + L^z dw) \cdot$$

$$\left(\frac{1}{1 - \frac{t_w \cdot w}{w_d} \left[\varepsilon^s - \frac{1}{(t_w dw + w dt_w)} \left(\varepsilon^{sH} + \frac{w_d}{L^s} \frac{\partial L^s}{\partial m} L^z\right) dw\right]}\right) + L^z dw. \tag{A.25}$$

If $dw = 0$, i.e., if demand for labor is perfectly elastic, then the MCPF reduces to equation (4.2). This is most easily seen from equation (A.24). However, the expression is difficult to interpret if the market wage adjusts. If both elasticities in (A.25) are positive, and w increases, then it is unclear whether the MCPF exceeds one or not. The first term within square brackets in the denominator appears with a minus sign, while the second positive term appears with a positive sign, and the final term is negative, provided labor is normal (but expected to be small because L^z/L^s is a small number). If the market wage increases, the considered project has an additional upfront cost. However, $L^z dw$ also benefits the representative agent, as reflected by the final term in (A.25).

If $L^s(w_d, m) = L(w) + L^z$, the change in the market wage caused by the change in z financed by a change of the income tax becomes:

$$\frac{\partial L^s}{\partial w_d}\left[(1 - t_w)\frac{dw}{dt_w} - w\right] - \frac{\partial L^s}{\partial m}L\frac{\partial w}{\partial t_w} = \frac{\partial L}{\partial w}\frac{dw}{dt_w} + \frac{dL^z}{dt_w}, \tag{A.26}$$

where L^z is viewed as an increasing function of the income tax, and T is kept constant. After some calculations, one obtains:

$$\frac{dw}{dt_w} = \frac{\frac{w_d}{L^s}\left(\frac{\partial L^s}{\partial w_d}w + \frac{dL^z}{dt_w}\right)}{\frac{w_d}{L^s}\left(\frac{\partial L^{sH}}{\partial w_d} - \frac{\partial L^s}{\partial w_d}t_w - \frac{\partial L}{\partial w} + \frac{\partial L^s}{\partial m}L^z\right)} = \frac{\varepsilon^s + \frac{w_d dL^Z}{L^s dt_w}}{\varepsilon^{sH} - t_w \cdot \varepsilon^s - \frac{w_d}{w}\varepsilon^d + \frac{w_d\partial L^s}{L^s\partial m}L^Z} \tag{A.27}$$

where the income effects sum to zero, explaining why a Hicksian labor supply function appears also here. If labor is normal, then $0 < \varepsilon^S < \varepsilon^{sH}$ due to a negative income effect (and $t_w \cdot \varepsilon^s < \varepsilon^s$ because the tax rate is less than one), while $\varepsilon^d < 0$. Hence, the denominator is positive if the final income effect is small (as is reasonably the case because L^d/L^s is a small number). Then, the market wage increases as the proportional labor tax is increased. Ceteris paribus, the absolute value of the numerator is larger, and the absolute value of the denominator is smaller than if $L^z = dL^z = 0$. Hence, the increase in L^z is likely to add to the wage increase.

Equations (A.25) and (A.27) illustrate that mechanically applying a standard MCPF on a project might produce biased results. In other words, deriving the MCPF without a project, multiplying the upfront cost of a project by the so-defined MCPF, and estimating (A.27) without the project could result in a flawed economic evaluation. The same conclusion follows if the considered project uses a produced good, say x, as input.

A.6 A General Equilibrium MCPF

In Subsection 5.11, a general equilibrium variation of the MCPF is stated. To arrive at this variation, one differentiates the government's budget constraint to obtain:

$$dT - t\frac{\partial x^d}{\partial m}dT + t\frac{\partial x^d}{\partial q}dp + t\frac{\partial x^d}{\partial w_d}dw + t\frac{\partial x^d}{\partial m}d\pi - wdL^z - L^z dw = 0. \quad \text{(A.28)}$$

Thus, one obtains:

$$-dT = \left(t\frac{\partial x^d}{\partial q}dp + t\frac{\partial x^d}{\partial w_d}dw + t\frac{\partial x^d}{\partial m}d\pi - wdL^z - L^z dw \right) \frac{1}{1 - t\frac{\partial x^d}{\partial m}}, \quad \text{(A.29)}$$

where the final term (to the right of the right-hand side parenthesis) is the familiar multiplier.

A.7 A Simple Intertemporal Extension

Subsection 6.2 provides a simple intertemporal extension of the model considered previously. The government aims to maximize social welfare subject to its intertemporal present value budget constraint. The Lagrangian is stated as follows:

$$F(.) = V(z_1, z_2, q_{11}, q_{21}, w_1, w_2 m)$$

$$+ \lambda \cdot \left(t_{11} \cdot x_{11}^d + t_{21} \cdot x_{21}^d - w_1 \cdot L_1^z - w_2 \cdot L_2^z \right), \quad \text{(A.30)}$$

where $q_{\tau 1} = p_{\tau 1} + t_{\tau 1} = \left(p_{\tau 1}^N + t_{\tau 1}^N \right) \cdot (1+r)^{\tau-1}, w_\tau = w_\tau^N \cdot (1+r)^{\tau-1}$, for $\tau = 1, 2,$ a superscript N refers to a nominal relative price in a period, $t_w = T = 0,$ and the commodity that acts as numéraire is suppressed. First-order conditions for an interior solution include:

$$\frac{\partial F}{\partial t_{11}} = -V_m \cdot x_{11}^d + \lambda \cdot x_{11}^d \left(1 + \frac{t_{11}}{x_{11}^d}\frac{\partial x_{11}^d}{\partial q_{11}} + \frac{t_{21}}{x_{11}^d}\frac{\partial x_{21}^d}{\partial q_{11}} \right) = 0,$$

$$\frac{\partial F}{\partial t_{21}} = -V_m \cdot x_{21}^d + \lambda \cdot x_{21}^d \left(1 + \frac{t_{21}}{x_{21}^d}\frac{\partial x_{21}^d}{\partial q_{21}} + \frac{t_{11}}{x_{21}^d}\frac{\partial x_{11}^d}{\partial q_{21}} \right) = 0,$$

$$\frac{\partial F}{\partial z_\tau} = V_{z_\tau} - \lambda \cdot w_\tau \frac{\partial L_\tau^z}{\partial z_\tau} = 0; \quad \tau = 1, 2. \quad \text{(A.31)}$$

Thus, at the second-best optimum, λ/V_m equals one over the expression within parentheses in the first and the second lines in (A.31). The implication is that the present value MCPF must be constant across time. Moreover, at the second-best optimum, in each period, the public good should be provided in such a quantity that the present value marginal WTP, i.e., V_{z_τ}/V_m, is equal to the direct present value marginal cost multiplied by the common or time-independent present value MCPF. Thus, social welfare can be improved beyond what equation (6.14) might seem to suggest by adjusting provision until the condition stated in the final line of equation (A.31) holds for both periods. It is straightforward to generalize the approach to an arbitrary number of periods.

References

Acheson, J., Stanley, B., Kennedy, S., & Morgenroth, E. L. W. (2018). *The Elasticity of Taxable Income*. Dublin: Department of Finance.

An, Z. (2023). On the marginal cost of public funds: The implications of charitable giving and warm glow. *Fiscal Studies: The Journal of Applied Public Economics*, 44(3), 299–307.

Arrow, K. J., & Hahn, F. H. (1971). *General Competitive Analysis*. Amsterdam: North-Holland.

Arrow, K. J., & Lind, R. C. (1970). Uncertainty and the evaluation of public investment decisions. *American Economic Review*, 60, 364–78.

Atkinson, A. B., Arrow, K., & Arnott, R. (1997). *Public Economics: Selected Papers by William Vickrey*. Cambridge: Cambridge University Press.

Auerbach, A. J., & Hines, J. Jr. (2002). Taxation and economic efficiency. In A. J. Auerbach & M. Feldstein, eds., *Handbook of Public Economics*, 1st ed., Volume 3, chapter 21, pp. 1347–421, Amsterdam, North-Holland: Elsevier.

Auriol, E., & Warlters, M. (2009). *The Marginal Cost of Public Funds and Tax Reform in Africa*. TSE WP 09–110, Toulouse School of Economics.

Auriol, E., & Warlters, M. (2012). The marginal cost of public funds and tax reform in Africa. *Journal of Development Economics*, 97(1), 58–72.

Ballard, C. L., & Fullerton, D. (1992). Distortionary taxation and the provision of public goods. *Journal of Economic Perspectives*, 6, 117–31.

Barone, E. (1912). Il ministro della produzione nello stato collettivista. *Giornale degli Economisti e Rivista di Statistica*, 37, 267–93.

Barrios, S., Pycroft, J., & Saveyn, B. (2013). *The Marginal Cost of Public Funds in the EU: The Case of Labour versus Green Taxes*. Working Paper No. 35, European Commission.

Bastani, S. (2023). *The Marginal Cost of Public Funds: A Brief Guide*. Institute for Evaluation of Labour Market and Education Policies, Working Paper No. 14.

Beaud, M. (2008). Le coût social marginal des fonds publics en France. *Annales d'Économie et de Statistique*, 90, 215–232.

Bessho, S., & Hayashi, M. (2013). Estimating the SMCPF of public funds: A microdata approach. *Public Finance Review*, 41(3), 360–85.

Bjertnaes, G. (2015). *Social Security Transfers and the Marginal Cost of Public Funds*. CESifo Working Paper Series No. 5689.

Boadway, R. W., & Bruce, N. (1984). *Welfare Economics*. Oxford: Basil Blackwell.

Boadway, R., & Keen, M. (1993). Public goods, self-selection and optimal income taxation. *International Economic Review*, 34, 463–78.

Boardman, A. E., Greenberg, D. H., Vining, A. R., & Weimer, D. L. (2018). *Cost-Benefit Analysis: Concepts and Practice*, 5th ed., Cambridge: Cambridge University Press.

Boardman, A. E., Greenberg, D. H., Vining, A. R., & Weimer, D. L. (2020). Efficiency without apology: Consideration of the marginal excess tax burden and distributional impacts in benefit–cost Analysis. *Journal of Benefit–Cost Analysis*, 11(3), 457–78.

Boehne, E. G. (1968). "Excess Burden" in Taxation: 75 Years of Controversy. *The American Economist*, 12(2), 22–37.

Bos, F., van der Pol, T., & Romijn, G. (2019). Should benefit–cost analysis include a correction for the marginal excess burden of taxation? *Journal of Benefit–Cost Analysis*, 10(3), 379–403. https://doi.org/10.1017/bca.2019.11.

Boyd, S., & Vandenberghe, L. (2004). *Convex Optimization*. Cambridge: Cambridge University Press.

Brent, R. J. (2006). *Applied Cost–Benefit Analysis*, 2nd ed., Cheltenham: Edward Elgar.

Brent, R. J. (2023). Use of distributional weights in cost–benefit analysis revisited. *Applied Economics*, 56(29), 3485–98.

Campbell, H. F., & Bond, K. A. (1997). The cost of public funds in Australia. *Economic Record*, 73(220), 22–34.

Chetty, R., Looney, A., & Kroft, K. (2009). Salience and taxation: Theory and evidence. *The American Economic Review*, 99(4), 1145–77.

Christiansen, V. (2007). Two approaches to determine public good provision under distortionary taxation. *National Tax Journal*, 60(1), 25–43.

Cuddington, J. T., Johansson, P.-O., & Löfgren, K.-G. (1984). *Disequilibrium Macroeconomics in Open Economies*. Oxford: Basil Blackwell.

Dahlby, B. (2008). *The Marginal Cost of Public Funds: Theory and Applications*. Cambridge, MA: The MIT Press.

Dahlby, B., & Ferede, E. (2012). The effects of tax rate changes on tax bases and the marginal cost of public funds for Canadian provincial governments. *International Tax and Public Finance*, 19(6), 844–83.

Dahlby, B., & Ferede, E. (2018). The marginal cost of public funds and the Laffer curve: Evidence from the Canadian provinces. FinanzArchiv: *Public Finance Analysis*, 74(2), 173–99.

Debreu, G. (1959). *Theory of Value. An Axiomatic Analysis of Economic Equilibrium*. New York: John Wiley & Sons.

de Rus, G. (2021). *Introduction to Cost–Benefit Analysis*. 2nd ed. Cheltenham: Edward Elgar.

Diamond, P. A. (1975). A many-person Ramsey tax rule. *Journal of Public Economics*, 4(4), 335–42.

Diamond, P. A. (1998). Optimal income taxation: An example with a U-shaped pattern of optimal marginal tax rates. *American Economic Review*, 88(1), 83–95.

Diamond, P., & Saez, E. (2011). The case for a progressive tax: From basic research to policy recommendations. *Journal of Economic Perspectives*, 25(4), 165–90.

Dixon, P., Honkatukia, J., & Rimmer, M. (2012). *The Marginal Cost of Funds from Different Taxes in Finland – An AGE Evaluation*. Conference papers 332273, Purdue University, Center for Global Trade Analysis, Global Trade Analysis Project.

Dupuit, J. (1844). De la mesure de l'utilite des travaux publics. *Annales des Ponts et Chausées*, 8, 29–65.

Elgin, C., Torul, O., & Turk, T. (2022). Marginal cost of public funds under the presence of informality. *Hacienda Pública Española / Review of Public Economics*, 241(2), 79–103.

European Commission. (2014). *Guide to Cost–Benefit Analysis of Investment Projects: Economic Appraisal Tool for Cohesion Policy 2014–2020*. Tech. rept. DG Regional Policy.

European Investment Bank (2023). *The Economic Appraisal of Investment Projects at the EIB*. 2nd ed. Luxembourg.

Figari, F., Gandullia, L., & Lezzi, E. (2018). Marginal cost of public funds: From the theory to the empirical application for the evaluation of the efficiency of the tax-benefit systems. *The B.E. Journal of Economic Analysis & Policy*, 18, 1–16. https://doi.org/10.1515/bejeap-2018-0132.

Fleurbaey, M., & Hammitt, J. K. (2024). The right numeraire or the just weights? How to make BCA rational and fair. *Journal of Benefit–Cost Analysis*, 15(1), 1–20.

Florio, M. (2014). *Applied Welfare Economics: Cost–Benefit Analysis of Projects and Policies*. New York: Routledge.

Fullerton, D. (1991). Reconciling recent estimates of the marginal welfare cost of taxation. *American Economic Review*, 81, 302–308.

Gahvari, F. (2006). On the marginal cost of public funds and the optimal provision of public goods. *Journal of Public Economics*, 90, 1251–62.

García, J. L., & Heckman, J. J. (2022). Three criteria for evaluating social programs. *Journal of Benefit-Cost Analysis*, 13(3), 281–86.

Groom, B., & Maddison, D. (2019). New estimates of the elasticity of marginal utility for the UK. *Environmental and Resource Economics*, 72, 1155–82.

Gruber, J., & Saez, E. (2002). The elasticity of taxable income: Evidence and implications. *Journal of Public Economics*, 84(1), 1–32.

Harberger, A. (1964). Taxation, resource allocation, and welfare. In NBER and the Brookings Institution, eds., *The Role of Direct and Indirect Taxes in the Federal Reserve System*, pp. 25–80. National Bureau of Economic Research. Princeton, NJ: Princeton University Press. http://www.nber.org/chapters/c1873.

Harberger, A. C., & Just, R. (2012). A conversation with Arnold Harberger. *Annual Review of Resource Economics*, 4, 1–26.

Harstad, B. (2020). Technology and time inconsistency. *Journal of Political Economy*, 128, 2653–89.

Hashimzade, N., & Myles, G. (2014). The marginal cost of public funds in growing economies. *Annals of Economics and Statistics*, 113/114, 11–36.

Hendren, N., & Sprung-Keyser, B. (2020). A unified welfare analysis of government policies. *Quarterly Journal of Economics*, 135(3),1209–318.

Hendren, N., & Sprung-Keyser, B. (2022). *The Case for Using the MVPF in Empirical Welfare Analysis*, National Bureau of Economic Research, WP 30029.

Hindriks, J., & Myles, G. D. (2005). *Intermediate Public Economics*. Cambridge, MA: MIT Press.

HM Treasury. (2011). *The Green Book. Appraisal and Evaluation in Central Government*. London: HMSO.

HM Treasury. (2022). *The Green Book (2022)*. Updated May 16, 2024. London: HMSO.

Holtsmark, B. (2019). *Is the Marginal Cost of Public Funds Equal to One?* Discussion Paper No. 893, Oslo: Statistics Norway, Research Department.

Jacobs, B. (2018). The marginal cost of public funds is one at the optimal tax system. *International Tax and Public Finance*, 25, 883–912.

Jaeger, W. K. (2024). Double dividend and environmental taxation. In T. Lundgren, M. Bostian, & S. Managi, eds., *Encyclopedia of Energy, Natural Resource, and Environmental Economics*. 2nd ed., pp. 31–37. Amsterdam: Elsevier,

Jehle, G. A., & Reny, P. J. (2011). *Advanced Microeconomic Theory*, 3rd ed., Harlow: Pearson Education.

Jensen, M. K. (2018). Distributional comparative statics. *The Review of Economic Studies*, 85(1), 581–610.

Johansson, P.-O. (2020). The 2018 reform of EU ETS: Consequences for project appraisal. *Journal of Environmental Economics and Policy*, 10(2), 214–21. https://doi.org/10.1080/21606544.2020.1835738.

Johansson, P.-O. (2021). On the evaluation of large projects in closed and open economies. *Journal of Transport Economics and Policy*, 55(3), 220–36.

Johansson, P.-O., & Kriström, B. (2016). *Cost–Benefit Analysis for Project Appraisal*. Cambridge: Cambridge University Press.

Johansson, P.-O., & Kriström, B. (2018). *Cost–Benefit Analysis*. Cambridge Elements. Elements in Public Economics. Cambridge: Cambridge University Press.

Johansson, P.-O., & Kriström, B. (2019). *On the Formulation of the Alternative Scenario in Cost–Benefit Analysis*. CERE Working Paper No. 6.

Johansson, P.-O., & Kriström, B. (2020). On the social opportunity cost of unemployment. *Journal of Economic Policy Reform*, 25(3), 229–39. https://doi.org/10.1080/17487870.2020.1785300.

Johansson, P.-O., & Kriström, B. (2022). Paying a premium for "green steel": Paying for an illusion? *Journal of Benefit–Cost Analysis*, 13, 383–93.

Johansson, P.-O, Kriström, B., & Falck, S. (2023). *Assessing the Welfare Effects of Electricity Tax Exemptions in General Equilibrium: The Case of Swedish Data Centers*. Stockholm: Swedish Agency for Growth Policy Analysis, WP 4, www.tillvaxtanalys.se.

Jorge-Calderón, D., & Johansson, P.-O. (2017). Emissions trading and taxes: An application to airport investment appraisals. *Journal of Transport Economics and Policy*, 51(4), 249–65.

Joseph, M. F. W. (1939). The excess burden of indirect taxation. *The Review of Economic Studies*, 6(3), 226–31.

Just, R. E., Hueth, D. L., & Schmitz, A. (2004). *The Welfare Economics of Public Policy: A Practical Approach to Project and Policy Evaluation*. Cheltenham: Edward Elgar.

Kaplow, L. (1996). The optimal supply of public goods and the distortionary cost of taxation. *National Tax Journal*, 49(4), 513–33.

Kaplow, L. (2004). On the (ir)relevance of distribution and labor supply distortion to government policy. *Journal of Economic Perspectives*, 18(4), 159–75.

Kaplow, L. (2008). *The Theory of Taxation and Public Economics*. Princeton: Princeton University Press.

Kleven, H. J., & Kreiner, C. T. (2003). *The Marginal Cost of Public Funds in OECD Countries: Hours of Work versus Labor Force Participation.* CESifo Working Paper Series No. 935.

Kleven, H. J., & Kreiner, C. T. (2006). The marginal cost of public funds: Hours of work versus labor force participation. *Journal of Public Economics*, 90(10–11), 1955–73.

Kotchen, M. J., & Levison, A. (2022). When can benefit–cost analyses ignore secondary markets? *Journal of Benefit–Cost Analysis*, 14(1), 114–40.

Kreiner, C. T., & Verdelin, N. (2012). Optimal provision of public goods: A synthesis. *Scandinavian Journal of Economics*, 114(2), 384–408.

Krutilla, K., & Graham, J. D. (2023). *Benefit-Cost Analysis of Air Pollution, Energy, and Climate Regulations.* Cambridge Elements. Elements in Public Economics. Cambridge: Cambridge University Press.

Laffont, J.-J. (1988). *Fundamentals of Public Economics.* Cambridge, MA: The MIT Press.

Layard, R., Mayraz, G., & Nickell, S. (2008). The marginal utility of income. *Journal of Public Economics*, 92(8–9), 1846–57.

Lindahl, E. (1958). Just taxation – A positive solution. In R. A. Musgrave & A. T. Peacock, eds., *Classics in the Theory of Public Finance*, pp. 168–176. International Economic Association Series. London: Palgrave Macmillan.

Loomis, J. B. (2011). Incorporating distributional issues into benefit cost analysis: Why, how, and two empirical examples using non-market valuation. *Journal of Benefit–Cost Analysis*, 2(1), 1–24, Article 5.

Lundholm, M. (2005). *Cost–Benefit Analysis and the Marginal Cost of Public Funds.* Research Papers in Economics 3, Stockholm University, Department of Economics.

Marshall, A. (1890). *Principles of Economics.* London: MacMillan.

McCarthy, D. (2024). *The Optimal Size and Financing of Government and the Dead-Weight Costs of Debt and Taxes.* https://ssrn.com/abstract=4953910 or http://dx.doi.org/10.2139/ssrn.4953910.

Mirrlees, J. A. (1971). An exploration in the theory of optimal income taxation. *Review of Economic Studies*, 38, 175–208.

Musgrave, A. (1987). Public finance. In J. Eatwell, M. Milgate, & P. Newman, eds., *The New Palgrave Dictionary of Economics*, pp. 1–11, London: MacMillan.

Myles, G. D. (1995). *Public Economics.* Cambridge: Cambridge University Press.

Nesticò, A., Maselli, G., Ghisellini, P., & Ulgiati, S. (2023). A dual probabilistic discounting approach to assess economic and environmental impacts. *Environmental and Resource Economics*, 85, 239–65.

Pigou, A. C. (1948). *A Study in Public Finance*. 3rd ed., London: Macmillan.

Piketty, T., & Saez, E. (2013). Optimal labor income taxation. In A. J. Auerbach, R. Chetty, M. Feldstein, & E. Saez, eds., *Handbook of Public Economics*, pp. 391–474, 5th Vol. Amsterdam: North-Holland.

Ramsey, F. (1927). A contribution to the theory of taxation. *Economic Journal*, 37, 47–61.

Rosendahl, K. E. (2019). EU ETS and the waterbed effect. *Nature Climate Change*, 9, 734–35.

Saez, E. (2001). Using elasticities to derive optimal income tax rates. *Review of Economic Studies*, 68(1), 205–29.

Saez, E., Slemrod, J., & Giertz, S. H. (2012). The elasticity of taxable income with respect to marginal tax rates: A critical review. *Journal of Economic Literature*, 50(1), 3–50.

Samuelson, P. A. (1954). The pure theory of public expenditure. *Review of Economics and Statistics*, 36, 387–89.

Sandmo, A. (1998). Redistribution and the marginal cost of public funds. *Journal of Public Economics*, 70(3), 365–82.

Slemrod, J., & Yitzhaki, S. (2001). Integrating expenditure and tax decisions: The marginal cost of funds and the marginal benefit of projects. *National Tax Journal*, 54(2), 189–201.

Smith, A. (1776). *An Inquiry into the Nature and Causes of the Wealth of Nations*. London: W. Strahan and T. Cadell.

Smith, K. (2022). *The Economics of Environmental Risk Information, Perception and Valuation*. Cheltenham: Edward Elgar.

Sørensen, P. B. (2011). *Calculating the Deadweight Loss from Taxation in a Small Open Economy - A General Method with an Application to Sweden*. EPRU Working Paper Series, No. 2011–03. Economic Policy Research Unit (EPRU), University of Copenhagen.

Sørensen, P. B. (2014). Calculating the deadweight loss from taxation in a small open economy – A general method with an application to Sweden. *Journal of Public Economics*, 117, 115–24.

Spackman, M. (2023). The social discount rate and the cost of public funds: A search for more consistency and better practice. *Journal of Environmental Economics and Policy*, 13(2), 228–242. https://doi.org/10.1080/21606544.2023.2236062.

Stern, N. (1982). Optimum taxation with errors in administration. *Journal of Public Economics*, 17(2), 181–211.

Stokey, N. L., & Lucas, JR, R. E. with Prescott, E. C. (1989). *Recursive Methods in Economic Dynamics*. Cambridge, MA: Harvard University Press.

Strand, J. (2009*). "Revenue Management" Effects Related to Financial Flows Generated by Climate Policy*. The World Bank Policy Research Working Paper No. 5053.

Strotz, R. H. (1955). Myopia and inconsistency in dynamic utility maximization. *Review of Economic Studies*, 23(3), 166–80.

Tuomala, M., (2016*). Optimal Redistributive Taxation*. Oxford: Oxford University Press.

US EPA. (2010). *Guidelines for Preparing Economic Analyses*. U.S. Environmental Protection Agency (EPA), Updated May 2014, Washington, DC. EPA 240-R-00-003.

Varian, H. R. (1992). *Microeconomic Analysis*, 3rd ed., New York: W. W. Norton.

Vásquez Cordano, A. L., & Balistreri, E. J. (2010). The marginal cost of public funds of mineral and energy taxes in Peru. *Resources Policy*, 35, 257–64.

Vickrey, W. S. (1955). Some implications of marginal cost pricing for public utilities. *The American Economic Review*, 45(2), 605–20.

Vickrey, W. S. (1968). Dupuit, Jules. In D. L. Sills, ed., *International Encyclopedia of the Social Sciences*, pp. 308–311. Vol. 4. Farmington Hills, Michigan.

Warlters, M., & Auriol, E. (2005). *The Marginal Cost of Public Funds in Africa*. World Bank Policy Research Working Paper No. 3679.

Willig, R. D. (1976). Consumer's surplus without apology. *American Economic Review*, 66, 589–97.

Acknowledgments

This Element draws on results by one of the authors contained in an annex to "Review of Shadow Prices. Report for the European Investment Bank," produced by the Institute for Transport Studies at the University of Leeds. No financial support has been received for the preparation of the manuscript. The views expressed are those of the authors and do not necessarily reflect those of the EIB or the University of Leeds. We are grateful to Massimo Florio, Chiara Del Bo, and an anonymous referee for useful comments and suggestions. However, any remaining errors and other flaws are our own responsibility.

For EU product safety concerns, contact us at Calle de José Abascal, 56–1°,
28003 Madrid, Spain or eugpsr@cambridge.org.